BLACK BOY

Richard Wright

WRITERS: Selena Ward, Ross Naughton

© 2002 by Spark Publishing

SPARKNOTES is a registered trademark of SparkNotes LLC

Spark Publishing
A Division of Barnes & Noble Publishing
120 Fifth Avenue
New York, NY 10011
www.sparknotes.com

ISBN-13: 978-1-5866-3397-4
ISBN-10: 1-5866-3397-X

Library of Congress information available upon request.

Please submit changes or report errors to www.sparknotes.com/errors.

Printed and bound in the United States.

1 3 5 7 9 10 8 6 4 2

INTRODUCTION: STOPPING TO BUY SPARKNOTES ON A SNOWY EVENING

Whose words these are you *think* you know.
Your paper's due tomorrow, though;
We're glad to see you stopping here
To get some help before you go.

Lost your course? You'll find it here.
Face tests and essays without fear.
Between the words, good grades at stake:
Get great results throughout the year.

Once school bells caused your heart to quake
As teachers circled each mistake.
Use SparkNotes and no longer weep,
Ace every single test you take.

Yes, books are lovely, dark, and deep,
But only what you grasp you keep,
With hours to go before you sleep,
With hours to go before you sleep.

Contents

CONTEXT

RICHARD WRIGHT WAS BORN on September 4, 1908, on a farm near the river town of Natchez, Mississippi. He was the first of two sons born to Nathan Wright, an illiterate tenant farmer, and Ella Wilson Wright, a teacher. When Richard was about five years old, his father abandoned the family to live with another woman. Trying to support herself and her two children—all the while trying to keep the rambunctious Richard under control—proved too stressful for Ella's delicate constitution, and she suffered a stroke that left her physically disabled for the rest of her life. His mother's health troubles shaped Wright's life in two significant ways. First, they meant that he had to work when his mother could not (which was often); this situation made his schooling intermittent at best. Second, it meant that Wright's living arrangements would change whenever his mother became too ill to care for her children. As such shifts occurred often, Wright had little opportunity to form coherent, nurturing, and meaningful relationships with family members or friends.

Despite his irregular schooling, Wright became an avid reader. When he was sixteen, he published a short story in a local black newspaper and began to harbor ambitions to write professionally. He faced considerable odds in this quest: his intensely religious household discouraged "idle" thoughts and creativity, while the dehumanizing Jim Crow South pronounced Wright and all black men unfit for anything but the lowliest work. When he moved himself and his family to Chicago in the late 1920s, circumstances were hardly more encouraging. As the Great Depression enveloped the country, Wright had to work a wide variety of stultifying and exhausting jobs to support his family. Nevertheless, he began to write seriously in private.

Wright entered the world of letters in 1933, when he began publishing poetry in various leftist and revolutionary magazines. He joined the Communist Party in 1934, writing for their publications and meeting many other disaffected writers, artists, and intellectuals who were also Party members. In 1937, Wright moved to New York and became Harlem editor of *The Daily Worker,* a Communist publication. The next eight years were the most triumphant of his life, as he published important essays such as "The

Ethics of Living Jim Crow," acclaimed stories like "Fire and Cloud," and two very successful novels: *Native Son* (1940) and the autobiographical *Black Boy* (1945).

This flurry of creative productivity did not overshadow Wright's political concerns, as he remained socially engaged with activist intellectuals for the rest of his life. He left the Communist Party in 1942 out of disapproval at what he considered the Party's soft stance on wartime racial discrimination. Wright left the United States in 1947, partly in protest against the deep flaws he discerned in American society. Settling with his wife and daughter in Paris, he became interested in existentialism, the philosophical movement that attempted to understand individual existence in the context of an unfathomable universe.

In Paris, Wright often socialized with Jean-Paul Sartre and Simone de Beauvoir, two influential thinkers and writers of the existentialist movement. He then began corresponding with Frantz Fanon, the West Indian social philosopher, in the 1950s. Wright published little of lasting value during these years, and when he died of a heart attack in 1960, it was clear that his writing career had peaked with *Native Son* and *Black Boy*. Nevertheless, the sheer power of those novels, and the thundering creativity of the years during which he produced them, ensured that Wright would be remembered not merely as an aspiring intellectual but as a powerful American artist.

Wright's autobiography, *Black Boy*, portrays his boyhood in the vicious Jim Crow South and his struggles with the Communist Party in Chicago. As such, a sensitive reading of this work depends on an understanding of its social and historical contexts. One of the primary contexts is the body of laws referred to as the "Jim Crow laws" after a crudely stereotypical character in white theater designed to degrade blacks for white entertainment.

Taking their cue from the infamous "separate but equal" ruling of *Plessy v. Ferguson* (1896), the Jim Crow laws mandated segregation of black from white not only in physical spaces such as restaurants, trains, movie theaters, and hospitals, but also in social arenas such as marriage. These laws effectively created two separate societies with highly unequal distributions of wealth. Primarily agricultural black populations were cast into extreme poverty and despair, enabling whites to take over the blacks' land and further exploit them as laborers on white-owned farms. As Wright learned when he traveled to New York, these laws were not exclusive to the

South. However, they were most devastating in the South, likely because the South's history of slavery made it especially difficult for whites to accept black emancipation.

Likewise, it is difficult to fully understand *Black Boy* without knowledge of American Communism in the 1930s and 1940s. These years saw the collapse of the stock market, industry stagnation, massive unemployment, and even famine in some parts of the United States. Many American intellectuals were disturbed by the capitalist mode of production, which, in their opinion, brought about these dreadful problems and then did very little to alleviate them. Communists believed in the dignity and agency of precisely those people who seemed to suffer the most. They claimed their political philosophy was based on a scientific model, and they advanced a theory of progress that emphasized not only equality, justice, and solidarity, but also conformity.

As many of these tenets of Communism appealed to human beings' noblest sentiments, the American Communist Party attracted many idealists, including Wright. As a black man, Wright was particularly interested in the convergence of confronting racism with Communism. Eventually, the American Communist Party saw the same internal bickering and division that plagued other American political organizations. The Party's increasingly authoritarian stance profoundly disappointed sensitive thinkers like Wright, who had joined the Party with firm hopes for a brighter future.

PLOT OVERVIEW

R EQUIRED TO REMAIN QUIET while his grandmother lies ill in bed, four-year-old Richard Wright becomes bored and begins playing with fire near the curtains, leading to his accidentally burning down the family home in Natchez, Mississippi. In fear, Richard hides under the burning house. His father, Nathan, retrieves him from his hiding place. Then, his mother, Ella, beats him so severely that he loses consciousness and falls ill.

Nathan abandons the family to live with another woman while Richard and his brother, Alan, are still very young. Without Nathan's financial support, the Wrights fall into poverty and perpetual hunger. Richard closely associates his family's hardship—and particularly their hunger—with his father and therefore grows bitter toward him.

For the next few years, Ella struggles to raise her children in Memphis, Tennessee. Her long hours of work leave her little time to supervise Richard and his brother. Not surprisingly, Richard gets into all sorts of trouble, spying on people in outhouses and becoming a regular at the local saloon—and an alcoholic—by the age of six. Ella's worsening health prevents her from raising two children by herself and often leaves her unable to work. During these times, Richard does whatever odd jobs a child can do to bring in some money for the family. School is hardly an option for him. At one point, the family's troubles are so severe that Ella must place her children in an orphanage for a few weeks.

Life improves when Ella moves to Elaine, Arkansas, to live with her sister, Maggie, and her sister's husband, Hoskins. Hoskins runs a successful saloon, so there is always plenty of food to eat, a condition that Richard greatly appreciates but to which he cannot accustom himself. Soon, however, white jealousy of Hoskins's business success reaches a peak, as local white men kill Hoskins and threaten the rest of his family. Ella and Maggie flee with the two boys to West Helena, Arkansas. There, the two sisters' combined wages make life easier than it had been in Memphis. After only a short time, however, Maggie flees to Detroit with her lover, Professor Matthews, leaving Ella the sole support of the family. Hard economic times return.

Times become even harder when a paralytic stroke severely inca-pacitates Ella. Richard's grandmother brings Ella, Richard, and Alan to her home in Jackson, Mississippi. Ella's numerous siblings convene in Jackson to decide how to care for their ailing sister and her two boys. The aunts and uncles decide that Alan, Richard's brother, will live with Maggie in Detroit. Ella will remain at home in Jackson. Richard, given the freedom to choose which aunt or uncle to live with, decides to take up residence with Uncle Clark, as Clark lives in Greenwood, Mississippi, not far from Jackson. Soon after he arrives at Clark's house, Richard learns from a neighbor that a young boy had died years ago in the same bedroom Richard now occupies. Too terrified to sleep, Richard successfully pleads to be returned to his grandmother's home.

Back at Granny's, Richard once again faces the familiar problem of hunger. He also faces a new problem: Granny's incredibly strict religious regimen. Granny, a Seventh-Day Adventist, sees her strong-willed, dreamy, and bookish grandson as terribly sinful, and she struggles mightily to reform him. Another of Richard's aunts, Addie, soon joins the struggle against Richard's defiance. Richard's obsession with reading and his lack of interest in religion make his home life an endless conflict. Granny forces him to attend the reli-gious school where Aunt Addie teaches.

One day in class, Aunt Addie beats Richard for eating walnuts, though it was actually the student sitting in front of Richard who had been eating the nuts, not Richard. When Addie tries to beat Richard again after school that day, he fends her off with a knife. Similar scenes recur with frustrating frequency over the following months and years. One time, Richard dodges one of Granny's back-hand slaps, causing her to lose her balance and injure herself in a fall off the porch. Addie tries to beat Richard for this incident, but he again fends her off with a knife. Later, another of Richard's uncles, Tom, comes to live with the family. One morning, Tom asks Richard what time it is and thinks Richard responds in a sassy manner. He tries to beat Richard for his supposed insolence, but the boy fends him off with razor blades.

Meanwhile, Richard picks his way through school. He delights in his studies—particularly reading and writing—despite a home climate hostile to such pursuits. To the bafflement and scorn of everyone, he writes and publishes in a local black newspaper a story titled "The Voodoo of Hell's Half-Acre." He graduates from the ninth grade as valedictorian, giving his own speech despite the insistence of his principal, friends, and family that he give a school-sanctioned speech to appease the white audience.

As Richard enters the adult working world in Jackson, he suffers many frightening, often violent encounters with racism. In the most demoralizing of these encounters, two white Southerners, Pease and Reynolds, run Richard off his job at an optical shop, claiming that such skilled work is not meant for blacks. Richard is upset because the white Northerner who runs the company, Mr. Crane, has hired Richard specifically for the purpose of teaching a black man the optical trade, but then does little to actually help defend Richard against his racist employees.

As his despair grows, Richard resolves to leave for the North as soon as possible. He becomes willing to steal in order to raise the cash necessary for the trip. After swindling his boss at a movie theater, selling stolen fruit preserves, and pawning a stolen gun, Richard moves to Memphis, where the atmosphere is safer and where he can make his final preparations to move to Chicago.

In Memphis, Richard has the seeming good fortune of finding a kind, generous landlady, Mrs. Moss, who determines that he must marry her daughter, Bess. Richard does not take to Bess, so his living situation is awkward until Mrs. Moss comes to terms with the fact that her daughter will never be Richard's wife. Richard takes a job at another optical shop, where Olin, a seemingly benevolent white coworker, plays mind games with Richard and Harrison, another young black worker, in an attempt to get them to kill each other. These strategies culminate in a grotesque boxing match between Richard and Harrison.

Another white coworker in the optical shop, Falk, is genuinely benevolent and lets Richard use his library card to check out books that otherwise would be unavailable to him. Richard begins reading obsessively and grows more determined to write. His mother, brother, and Maggie soon join him in Memphis. They all decide that Richard and Maggie will go to Chicago immediately and that the other two will follow in a few months.

In Chicago, Richard continues to struggle with racism, segregation, poverty, and with his own need to cut corners and lie to protect himself and get ahead. He suppresses his own morals, forcing himself to work at a corrupt insurance agency that takes advantage of poor blacks. He also works in a café and for a couple of well-meaning Jewish storeowners, the Hoffmans, in a whites-only neighborhood. Irresponsibly, Richard soon quits to try to get a job in the post office.

As the Great Depression forces him and millions of others out of work, Richard begins to find Communism appealing, especially its emphasis on protecting the oppressed. He becomes a Communist Party member because he thinks that he can help the Party cause with his writing, finding the language that can promote the Party's cause to common people.

Meanwhile, Richard works various jobs through federal relief programs. When he begins writing for leftist publications, he takes positions with federal theater companies and with the Federal Writers' Project. To his mounting dismay, he finds that, like any other group, the Communist Party is beset with human fears and foibles that constantly frustrate its own ends. Richard's desire to write biographical sketches of Communists and his tendency to criticize Party pronouncements earn him distrust, along with the titles "intellectual" and "Trotskyite." After a great deal of political strife and slander that culminates in his being physically assaulted during a May Day parade, Richard leaves the Party. Unfazed by the failure of his high hopes, he remains determined to make writing his link to the world.

CHARACTER LIST

Richard Wright Author, narrator, and protagonist of *Black Boy*. Richard is an unpredictable bundle of contradictions: he is timid yet assured, tough yet compassionate, enormously intelligent yet ultimately modest. Passive-aggressive as a young boy, Richard either says very little or becomes melodramatic and says too much. Growing up in an abusive family environment in the racially segregated and violent American South, Richard finds his salvation in reading, writing, and thinking. He grows up feeling insecure about his inability to meet anyone's expectations, particularly his family's wish that he accept religion. Even though he remains isolated from his environment and peers, at the autobiography's end Richard has come to accept himself. *Black Boy* testifies to his gifted observational powers and his ability to reflect upon the psychological struggles facing black Americans.

Ella Wright Richard's mother. Tough on Richard and certainly unafraid to administer a beating when she believes it is appropriate, Ella nevertheless loves her son and is the person most resembling an advocate in his life. Despite falling into ill health and becoming partially paralyzed, she maintains an optimistic outlook on life.

Granny Richard's maternal grandmother. Austere and unforgiving, Granny is a very strict Seventh-Day Adventist and runs her household accordingly. She thinks Richard is sinful, has little tolerance for his antics, and is inclined to demonstrate her disapproval with a quick backhanded slap across his mouth. Like her husband, Richard Wilson, Granny is the child of slaves. Due to her partially white ancestry, she looks somewhat white.

Alan   Richard's younger brother. Born Leon Alan Wright, he goes by the name Alan. Alan does not contribute much to the story of *Black Boy*: a few times, he limply objects to something naughty that Richard is planning to do, like burn straws in a fireplace or hang a kitten. In this sense, he serves as one of Richard's critics.

Aunt Addie One of Ella's sisters. Addie lives at home with Granny in Jackson, Mississippi. She shares her mother's spite for Richard and tries not to miss any opportunity to beat or humiliate him. She shares Granny's intense religious nature and teaches at a religious school that Richard briefly attends.

Grandpa   Richard's maternal grandfather and a former soldier in the Union Army during the Civil War. Sour and remote, Grandpa is forever bitter that a clerical error has deprived him of his war pension. He keeps his distance from the family but is occasionally trotted out to discipline Richard. Grandpa keeps a loaded gun by his bed, as he believes that Civil War hostilities could resurface at any moment.

Nathan Wright Richard's father. Although Nathan is physically intimidating and frequently beats Richard, he abandons the family and proves to be simple, weak, and pathetic.

Aunt Maggie Ella's sister. Maggie sporadically lives with Ella, Richard, and his brother, and is Richard's favorite aunt.

Uncle Hoskins Maggie's first husband. Uncle Hoskins is a friendly man, but loses Richard's trust when he pretends to drive his buggy into the river to frighten Richard. Local whites murder Hoskins when they grow jealous of his profitable saloon.

"Professor" Matthews Maggie's second husband. The "Professor" is an outlaw and, when he begins courting Maggie, he visits only at night. After he apparently kills a white woman, he and Maggie flee to Detroit. Several years after that, he deserts Maggie.

Uncle Clark One of Ella's brothers. Uncle Clark briefly houses Richard after his mother becomes ill. Clark is a just, upright man who seems genuinely concerned for Richard's welfare, although perhaps a little strict.

Uncle Tom Another of Ella's brothers. Like Aunt Addie, Uncle Tom finds Richard particularly galling and seems to leap at any opportunity to beat or ridicule him.

Ella, the schoolteacher A young schoolteacher who briefly rents a room in Granny's house. Bookish and dreamy, she introduces Richard to the imaginative pleasures of fiction by telling him the story of *Bluebeard and His Seven Wives*. Granny, however, views Ella's stories as sinful and effectively forces Ella to move out.

Griggs One of Richard's boyhood friends. Griggs, like Richard, is intelligent, but he has a sense of when blacks need to abide by the rules—a sense Richard lacks. Griggs displays the compassionate concern of a true friend when he advises Richard on how to survive in the racist white world.

Pease and Reynolds Two white Southerners who run Richard off his job at the optical shop in Jackson, Mississippi. Though technically two characters, Pease and Reynolds are unified in their bestial treatment of Richard and essentially operate as one.

Mr. Crane A white Northerner who runs the optical shop where Richard works. Mr. Crane is a fair and unprejudiced man, who is sad to see Richard go when Pease and Reynolds run him off the job.

Olin   A white Southerner at Richard's job at the optical shop in Memphis, Tennessee. Racist and destructive, Olin pretends to be Richard's friend but then tells lies in an attempt to get Richard and Harrison to kill each other.

Harrison A young black man who works at a rival optical shop in Memphis. The fight between Richard and Harrison demonstrates that racism's power to instill fear in blacks is so great that it can lead two black men who truly like each other to fight each other viciously.

The Hoffmans White Jewish shopkeepers who employ Richard in Chicago. The Hoffmans treat Richard with genuine respect and care, but Richard assumes that because they are white they will act just like most Southern whites. The Hoffmans help Richard begin his journey toward accepting some well-meaning white people, even though he treats them poorly at the time.

Shorty The black elevator man in the building in Memphis where Richard works. Shorty is witty, intelligent, and has a sense of pride in his race. However, much to Richard's horror, Shorty engages in supremely demeaning behavior to earn money.

Falk A white Irish Catholic worker at the optical shop in Memphis. In stark counterpoint to Olin, Falk does not explicitly profess to be Richard's friend, but he proves to be a genuine friend by letting Richard borrow his library card to obtain books from the whites-only library. When Falk learns that Richard is moving to Chicago, the quick smile he flashes suggests that he is pleased Richard is moving on to a better life.

Comrade Young An escapee from a mental institution who suddenly appears at a meeting of the John Reed Club, a revolutionary artists' organization Richard joins in Chicago. Comrade Young illustrates the vulnerability of the Communist Party to fraudulent acts by individuals.

Ross   A black Communist whom Richard wishes to profile for his series of biographical sketches. Ross is somewhat uneasy around Richard, fearing Richard's deviations from Party doctrine.

Ed Green A high-ranking black Communist suspicious of Richard's interviews with Ross. Green's rough, peremptory, and authoritative manner alienates Richard.

ANALYSIS OF MAJOR CHARACTERS

RICHARD WRIGHT

Richard's most essential characteristic is his tremendous belief in his own worth and capabilities. This belief frequently renders him willful, stubborn, and disrespectful of authority, putting him at odds with his family and with those who expect him to accept his degraded position in society. Because almost everyone in Richard's life thinks this way, he finds himself constantly punished for his nonconformity with varying degrees of physical violence and emotional isolation. Though Richard shows signs of insecurity, inferiority, and shame around some whites, his self-assurance seems largely invulnerable, and his punishing childhood only serves to convince him of his own right to succeed in the world. Moreover, Richard's difficult and isolating experiences as a child fuel his intensely powerful imagination, his love of reading and writing, and his will to make his life feel meaningful through writing about his environment.

Wright paints himself in several different shades throughout the course of *Black Boy*. As a young boy, Richard is simply unable to believe the publicly accepted notions that his blackness, lack of religion, and intellectual curiosity make him inherently flawed. Rather, we find in Richard a character determined to live according to his own principles and willing to live with the consequences. This strong-willed nature, however, contrasts with Richard's powerless position in society—the low social status that comes with being black and poor. Starting off removed from society and his family, Richard must learn to educate himself. Much of this education stems from his experiences—in the homes of sharecroppers, as a black in the Jim Crow South, as a resident of the cramped apartments of Depression-era Chicago. There are clearly negative aspects to the character Richard develops, as we see him lie, steal, and turn violent numerous times in the book. In a sense, he is a victim of his poor upbringing—in both the black and white communities in the South; as a victim, he becomes contaminated by the oppressive forces working against him.

Despite his flaws, Richard remains intensely concerned with humanity, both in a universal sense and in the context of his concern for the individual people he meets on his journey. In this way, Richard overcomes the negative, debilitating, isolating aspects of his environment and channels them into a love for other people. He is an outsider who feels little connection to other people, yet who cares for these people nonetheless. Richard's traits do not exist in perfect harmony: at certain points, one trait will seem to dominate, only to give way to other traits at other times. However, because the character of Richard Wright so convincingly contains all these traits, albeit in imbalance, he has a self-contradictory appeal that transcends the simple biographical facts of his life.

ELLA WRIGHT

Richard's contentious relationship with his mother may be traced back to his early childhood, when Ella administers a beating that nearly kills him. This strife continues throughout Richard's early years, as he commits endless punishable offenses in a setting where his mother is often the only authority figure around to deliver punishment. Despite her sometimes brutal discipline, Ella is devoted to her children and is fiercely determined to raise them successfully after her husband abandons the family.

Ella shows a special tolerance and affection for Richard that we do not see in any of the other major characters. When Richard publishes "The Voodoo of Hell's Half-Acre," for example, the rest of the family attacks him, but Ella shows compassion through her concern that Richard's writing might make it hard for him to get a job. Similarly, Ella walks on her weak legs to give Richard a hug when she learns that he will get a job in defiance of Granny's and Addie's wishes, suggesting that she takes genuine delight in her son's success.

Much of the meaning of Ella's character lies in her illness, as she symbolizes those elements of life that are at once unpredictable, overwhelming, and unfair. In Chapter 3, Ella's suffering effectively becomes a symbol of everything wrong with the world for Richard. In a just universe, he concludes, the unfriendly and harmful people would be sick, and Ella would enjoy vigorous health, unimpeded in going about the business of raising her sons and earning a living. However, the reality is, of course, that Ella is constantly sick and suffering. In light of the seemingly cruel fate his mother endures, Richard finds it difficult to deny that the universe is unjust. The injustice he sees afflicting his mother mirrors the injustices he himself faces: poverty, hunger, a severely abridged education, and the mere fact of being black in the Jim Crow South. Taken together, these accidents of life constitute a major obstacle that Richard must overcome in order to live the life that he wants.

GRANNY, ADDIE, TOM, PEASE, REYNOLDS, OLIN, ED GREEN, BUDDY NEALSON

This list of supporting characters—a list that could easily be extended—may seem inconsistent. Indeed, there are plenty of reasons why black family members of Richard's do not belong in a list with white racists like Pease and Reynolds, and why city-dwelling black Communists like Ed Green and Buddy Nealson do not belong with the other characters either. With respect to Richard, though, all of these characters are part of the same group: they all ascribe to inflexible attitudes and beliefs that do not accommodate differing opinions from independently minded people like Richard.

In the cases of Granny and Addie, strict religious faith drives them to attack Richard at every turn because he fails to act like a good Seventh-Day Adventist. Tom's belief that young people should unthinkingly obey their elders rouses him to fury whenever Richard takes a justified stand against him. Pease, Reynolds, and Olin believe that black people exist merely for the service and sport of white people, leading them to treat Richard with shocking inhumanity. Finally, Ed Green and Buddy Nealson, who maintain that Communists should quietly march in step with the Party, vilify Richard as soon as he seems to be marching to a different drummer.

In short, these characters all deny Richard's worth as an individual. The American essayist Ralph Waldo Emerson wrote in *Self-Reliance* that "[s]ociety everywhere is in conspiracy against the manhood of every one of its members," in that the "base doctrine of the majority of voices usurps the place of the doctrine of the soul." Taken together, these characters represent the multitude of ways in which society "is in conspiracy against" Richard.

THEMES, MOTIFS & SYMBOLS

THEMES

Themes are the fundamental and often universal ideas explored in a literary work.

THE INSIDIOUS EFFECTS OF RACISM

Racism as a problem among individuals is a familiar topic in literature. *Black Boy,* however, explores racism not only as an odious belief held by odious people but also as an insidious problem knit into the very fabric of society as a whole. Wright portrays characters such as Olin and Pease as evil people, but also—and more chillingly—as bit players in a vast drama of hatred, fear, and oppression. For Richard, the true problem of racism is not simply that it exists, but that its roots in American culture are so deep it is doubtful whether these roots can be destroyed without destroying the culture itself.

More than simply an autobiography, *Black Boy* represents the culmination of Wright's passionate desire to observe and reflect upon the racist world around him. Throughout the work, we see Richard observe the deleterious effects of racism not only as it affects relations between whites and blacks, but also relations among blacks themselves. Wright entitles his work *Black Boy* primarily for the emphasis on the word "black": this is a story of childhood, but at every moment we are acutely aware of the color of Wright's skin. In America, he is not merely growing up; he is growing up black. Indeed, it is virtually impossible for Richard to grow up without the label of "black boy" constantly being applied to him.

Whites in the novel generally treat Richard poorly due to the color of his skin. Even more important, racism is so insidious that it prevents Richard from interacting normally even with the whites who *do* treat him with a semblance of respect (such as the Hoffmans or Mr. Crane) or with fellow blacks (such as Harrison). Perhaps the most important factor in Wright's specifically "black" upbringing, however, is the fact that he grows up among black people who are unable or unwilling to accept his individual personality and his gifts. Wright's critique of racism in America includes a critique of the black community itself—specifically the black folk community that is unable or unwilling to educate him properly. The fact that he has been kept apart from such education becomes clear to Richard when he recognizes his love of literature at a late age.

THE INDIVIDUAL VERSUS SOCIETY
Richard is fiercely individual and constantly expresses a desire to join society on his own terms rather than be forced into one of the categories that society wishes him to fill. In this regard, Richard struggles against a dominant white culture—both in the South and in the North—and even against his own black culture. Neither white nor black culture knows how to handle a brilliant, strong-willed, self-respecting black man. Richard perceives that his options are either to conform or to wilt. Needless to say, neither option satisfies him, so he forges his own middle path.

Richard defies these two unsatisfactory options in different ways throughout the novel. He defies them in Granny's home, where he lives without embracing its barren, mandatory spirituality. He defies these options at school, where the principal asserts that Richard must read an official speech or not graduate. He defies them in Chicago, where the Communist Party asserts that he will either act as they tell him to act or be expelled. Richard negates this final choice by leaving the Party of his own accord. As we see, Richard always rejects the call to conform. This rejection creates strife and difficulty, however—not because Richard thinks cynically about people and refuses to have anything more to do with them, but precisely because he does *not* take this approach. Though Richard wishes to remain an individual, he feels connected to the rest of humanity on a spiritual level. Therefore, as an artist, he must struggle to show compassion for communities that say they do not want him. It is a difficult task, but one that he learns to accept at the end of the novel.

THE REDEMPTIVE POWER OF ART
When Ella the schoolteacher furtively whispers to Richard the plot of *Bluebeard and His Seven Wives*, Richard becomes transfixed; he says that the story evokes his first "total emotional response." This trend continues throughout the novel, as a number of experiences in Richard's life prove eye-opening in the best sense, enabling him to become excited about his life and to feel that his life has texture,

meaning, and purpose. Such eye-opening experiences include Richard's hearing of the Bluebeard story, his reading of science-fiction and horror magazines, his penning of the story of the Indian maiden, his discovery of H. L. Mencken, his writing of "The Voodoo of Hell's Half-Acre," and his decision that he can use his writing to advance the cause of the Communist Party. These experiences all involve reading or some other use of his imaginative faculties, and all bolster his idea that life becomes meaningful through creative attempts to make sense of it. This is a core idea in the history of philosophy, first articulated by Schopenhauer, refined by Nietzsche, and then taken up by the existentialists, with whom Wright grew fascinated. Indeed, the writing of *Black Boy* itself, when seen as Wright's attempt to order the experiences of his life, is closely tied to this idea of the redemptive power of creativity.

MOTIFS

Motifs are recurring structures, contrasts, or literary devices that can help to develop and inform the text's major themes.

HUNGER

By frequently reminding us of the problem of his physical hunger, Wright emphasizes his hunger for other things as well—for literature, artistic expression, and engagement in social and political issues. Though there are indeed many instances in the novel when Richard does physically hunger for food, he eventually concludes that food is not as important as the other problems facing the world. He asserts that the world needs unity more than it needs to cure physical ills. Both Richard and the world have a more important need: understanding of and connection with one another. Physical hunger is merely a symbol of the larger emptiness Richard's brutal, inhumane life causes him to feel. Throughout the autobiography he exhibits a strong desire to carve out a richer, more satisfying existence by connecting with the world around him. Just as literal hunger works to undo itself by making a person want to eat, so the motif of hunger works in *Black Boy*. Richard's greater emotional and intellectual hunger serves as a sort of literary magnet that pulls us through the story, making us just as anxious to see Richard succeed as he is.

READING

Throughout the text, Richard seeks out reading with a passion that resembles a physical appetite. Indeed, these two sensations—the desire to read and the desire to eat—are closely allied. At times, this alliance breaks down and the two sensations flow together. In Chapter 5, for example, Richard catches the smell of meat frying in a neighbor's kitchen while he is reading. From his bookish day-dreams, Richard drifts into a fantasy of having plenty of meat to eat. There is also the image, in Chapter 15, of Richard simultaneously devouring food and Proust's novel *A Remembrance of Things Past*, hoping to flesh out his body and his writing. It is as if Proust is part of Richard's weight-gaining plan. This blurring of literary and physical appetite is most explicit when Richard remarks, "I lived on what I did not eat," suggesting that, at some level, reading takes the place of food. As such, reading works as a counterpoint to the motif of hunger in the novel. While hunger represents the spiritual and emotional emptiness within Richard, reading represents Richard's bread and water, giving him the energy he needs to persevere.

VIOLENCE

Richard is cursed, beaten, or slapped every time he stands up to Granny, Addie, or other elders, regardless of how justified he may be in doing so. When whites believe Richard is behaving unaccept-ably in their presence, they berate, slap, or manipulate him; in one instance, they smash a whiskey bottle in his face. When Richard acts out of line with the Communist Party, they denounce him and attempt to sabotage his career. Clearly, then, violence—which here means all the abuse, physical or mental, that Richard suffers—is a constant presence in *Black Boy*. Violence looms as an almost inevi-table consequence when Richard asserts himself, both in the family and in society.

However, violence takes over Richard's mind as well. Richard learns that he must demonstrate his violent power in order to gain respect and acceptance at school. Additionally, he reacts to his fam-ily's violent, overbearing treatment with violence of his own, wield-ing a knife against Addie, burning down the house, and so on. More broadly, violence infects the black community in general, whether from within or from the white community's imposed violence.

Perhaps the most important violent sequence in the novel occurs when Olin makes Richard and Harrison suspect each other of mur-derous intentions. Even though they acknowledge to each other that they mean each other no harm, they cannot escape the reality that the racist culture demands they fight viciously. One root of this violence between Richard and Harrison is Olin's feigned friendship toward each of the men. Thus, we come to see that violence in a racist world often goes beyond physical attacks.

SYMBOLS

> *Symbols are objects, characters, figures, or colors used to represent abstract ideas or concepts.*

ELLA'S INFIRMITY

In Renaissance and Gothic literature, a deformity or some other physical impairment often serves as an outward sign of an unhealthy or evil soul. This kind of symbolism implies that the universe is a sensible place, as an evil soul is rewarded with a mangled body. In *Black Boy*, however, the opposite is true. Richard's mother, Ella, is one of the few people in the novel—and the only person in the entire family—who seems genuinely concerned for Richard's welfare. If anyone in the novel has a truly good, saintlike soul, it is Ella. However, she is beset with incurable ailments and paralytic legs. Other family members, meanwhile, have abundant strength, which they frequently use to beat Richard for trivial offenses. In this context, Ella's infirmity symbolizes for Richard the unfair and random nature of the universe.

THE OPTICAL SHOP IN MEMPHIS

In the microcosm of the optical shop in Memphis, Olin represents the Southern white racists willing to terrorize black people for the sake of amusement, while Falk represents those Southern whites who genuinely sympathize with black people and who are willing to help them. Shorty represents the black workers who pander to whites but inwardly retain their racial and personal pride. The building's unnamed porter, with his daily wail about having to work in the same place day in and day out, represents the more embittered black workers of the South. Several Ku Klux Klan members and Jews also populate the office. As such, the Memphis optical shop is a microcosm of racial stratification in the South. Wright concentrates the racial dynamics of the region in one physical space in order to show that people who think they are different from or better than their peers are actually integrally connected to them.

Summary & Analysis

Part I (Southern Night): Chapter 1

Summary

Frustrated by his mother's order to remain quiet, four-year-old Richard Wright is bored out of his mind in his grandparents' house in Natchez, Mississippi. With nothing better to do, Richard plays with a broom, lighting stray straws in the fireplace and watching them burn. He then decides to set the curtains on fire to see what they look like when they burn. The fire rages out of control, and the terrified Richard runs out of the room. Fearing punishment, he hides under the burning house until his father, Nathan, retrieves him. Richard's mother, Ella, then lashes him until he loses consciousness, knocking him into a delusional fever for several days. Wright then muses, in a stretch of intensely descriptive writing, on his fantastical and sentimental reflections upon the world around him. Richard recovers from his fever and moves with his family to Memphis, Tennessee. His father, Nathan, works as a night porter in a drugstore and sleeps during the day. One morning, Richard and his brother, playing with a noisy stray kitten they have found outside, wake Nathan. The kitten will not go away. In frustration, Nathan shouts, "Kill that damn thing!" Though Richard knows that his father does not really want them to kill the cat, he resents his father's shouting and domineering behavior, and resolves to take his order literally. Richard hangs the kitten. This act angers Nathan, but Richard reminds him of his words and feels triumphant. Ella, infuriated with her son, punishes him by forcing him to bury the kitten alone that night, which fills him with shame and terror.

Nathan soon abandons the family to live with another woman. Without his financial support, Ella and her children are left constantly hungry. When Richard begs his mother for food, she responds by informing him that he no longer has a father, which leads Richard to develop a bitter association between his father and hunger. Later, a gang of boys attack and rob Richard when Ella sends him to the grocery store. Ella sends Richard a second time, but the boys only rob him again. Finally, Ella arms Richard with a heavy stick and sends him along once more, telling him she will whip him if he comes back into the house without the groceries. Richard is terrified to be courting violence, but fights back with the stick when the gang again attacks him, managing to crack several of the boys on their heads. The boys run home to their parents, who come outside and threaten Richard. However, the emboldened Richard tells the parents that they will get a similar beating if they come after him.

Richard briefly amuses himself by hiding, with other young boys, behind a row of open-back outhouses to watch people relieve themselves. To keep her sons out of such trouble, Ella starts to take them along with her to the white household where she works as a cook. The constantly hungry Richard resents watching the white family digging into their plentiful food.

Richard soon finds a new form of amusement: peeping into a nearby saloon and laughing at the silliness of the drunks who go in and out. One customer eventually drags the frightened Richard inside the saloon, and the patrons give him drinks and money if he repeats various curse words. This activity becomes an obsession for Richard, and he soon becomes a six-year-old drunkard. Aware of his problem, Ella beats her son and pleads with him to stop, but she is unable to change his behavior. Ella finally stops Richard by leaving him and his brother in the care of an older black woman, who watches them very closely. Trapped under the woman's watch, Richard loses his taste for alcohol.

Richard gradually learns to read by leafing through children's books, and learns to count to one hundred when a benevolent deliveryman spends an hour teaching him numbers. His mind increasingly fills with relentless questions, Richard begins to vaguely understand that relations between white and black people are very tricky, but he cannot get anyone to discuss the matter openly with him. He also has trouble understanding the distinction between blacks and whites, as his grandmother, a black woman, looks somewhat white. When Richard hears a rumor that a white man beat a black boy in the neighborhood, he assumes that the man was the boy's father, believing that only parents have the right to beat children. Ella corrects her son's misunderstanding about the man and the boy, but she refuses to discuss the matter further, leaving Richard puzzled about white people and wondering why they would beat a black person.

Richard begins the first grade, but he is so terrified on the first day of school that he cannot speak. At recess a group of older boys teaches him the meanings of all the curse words he had been paid to repeat in the saloon. Eager to display this new knowledge, Richard races home after school and uses soap to write the curse words on every available window in the neighborhood. Ella, horrified, forces him to wash all the windows while the neighbors look on with pity and amusement.

Ella invites the preacher from the local black church over for a dinner of fried chicken. Richard is very excited about the relatively fancy meal, but Ella will not let Richard eat any of the chicken until he finishes his soup, which he is unable to do in his excitement for the meat. Increasingly distressed as he watches the preacher devour piece after piece of the precious chicken, Richard eventually runs out of the room, screaming that the preacher is going to eat everything. The preacher laughs, but Ella does not find Richard's dramatic actions amusing, and forbids him any more dinner.

Ella sues Nathan for child support, but Nathan successfully convinces the judge that he is already giving all the support he can. Richard notes that he does not hate his father but merely prefers not to see him or think of him at all. For this reason, Richard refuses his mother's requests that he go to his father's job and beg him for money.

Poverty forces Ella to place Richard and his brother in an orphanage for a month, where they eat two miserable meals per day and tend the lawn, pulling grass by hand. The orphanage director, Miss Simon, apparently takes a liking to Richard and asks him to help her blot envelopes in her office. Once in Miss Simon's office, however, Richard is paralyzed with an inexplicable fear and is unable to do anything she asks of him. Frustrated, Miss Simon drives Richard from her office. He decides to run away from the orphanage that night, and when he does so he gets lost. Richard encounters a white policeman, but he remembers the story of the white man beating the black boy and fears that the policeman will beat him. The policeman is friendly, however, and brings Richard back to the orphanage. Miss Simon promptly lashes Richard for running away.

Ella decides that the family should go to her sister Maggie's home in Elaine, Arkansas. She takes Richard out of the orphanage so that he can go to Nathan and plead for the money the family needs to make the journey. Predictably, Nathan claims that he has no money to give, and he seems amused by the idea that his children are going hungry. A slight altercation ensues, and Richard and his mother say harsh words to the irritatingly jolly Nathan and his mistress. Nathan then offers Richard a nickel, and though the boy wants to accept it, he refuses.

Richard muses that this meeting is the last time he would see his father for twenty-five years. When he next sees Nathan, the old man is nothing more than a poor, toothless sharecropper. Richard feels nothing but pity for Nathan as an old man, reflecting that whereas Nathan failed in his attempt to find a successful life in the city, Richard himself has done much better, and created a dramatically new life out of his humble origins.

ANALYSIS

Though it is essentially autobiographical, at times *Black Boy* does not resemble a conventional autobiography. Immediately following Richard's description of his almost-fatal illness, for example, Wright includes a lengthy passage of lyrical prose that details his sentimental responses to the natural environment. Phrases such as "the tantalizing melancholy in the tingling scent of burning hickory wood" and "the aching glory in masses of clouds burning gold and purple from an invisible sun" shift the focus of the narrative away from concrete facts and toward more nebulous depictions of Richard's imaginative mind. These phrases give human qualities to inanimate matter and contain highly subjective feelings that we typically associate with fiction and poetry. Because it contains such purely artistic passages in addition to concrete biographical information, *Black Boy* is often termed an autobiographical novel. Similar to Maya Angelou's *I Know Why the Caged Bird Sings*, Wright's novel strikes a creative compromise between fact and fiction—in part because the author wishes to describe events and ideas deeply embedded in the memories of early childhood.

One of Wright's central concerns in *Black Boy* is the insidious nature of racism in the United States—insidious because its roots and effects are very subtle. At first glance, Chapter 1 may not seem to explore this idea of racism very much at all. Though Richard resents the well-fed white family that employs his mother and fears the white policeman who returns him to the orphanage, these situations contain nothing that resembles outright racial conflict. Similarly, Richard's failed attempt to learn why a white man beats a black boy does not say anything overt about racism itself; it only seems to prove that Richard is interested in learning about race but is having difficulty doing so. Yet Wright strives to portray the subtle, sometimes even invisible workings of racism, and the events in Chapter 1 do contribute to this portrayal. In his encounters with the white family and the white policeman, Richard is already beginning to display a strong association between white people and the injustices of the world. This association is itself harmful because the young Richard already sees it as natural.

The fact that no one will answer Richard's questions about race relations reveals that Richard lives not only in a society of racist whites, but also in an environment that blacks themselves make worse for him. In a racist society, the oppressors fear curiosity among the oppressed, as curiosity eventually uncovers the lies that form the foundation of that oppression. The oppressors therefore use any means necessary to discourage such curiosity. Under the worst conditions of oppression, the oppressed even do the oppressors' dirty work for them by discouraging curiosity among their own ranks. Indeed, we see that Richard's family discourages his curiosity concerning racial matters. More broadly, blacks often try to discourage anyone who could cause trouble for the rest of the group by speaking out against injustice.

Richard's actions in Chapter 1 reveal a pattern of unpredictable—either passive-aggressive or over-reactive—behavior that hinders his ability to peacefully adapt to his surroundings. For example, when his parents force him to be silent, Richard burns down the house, resulting in a thorough beating. He rebels against his father's overbearing demeanor by killing a kitten, only angering his parents further. Richard overcomes his profound fear of the gang of boys by fiercely attacking them and threatening their parents. His quiet fascination with the saloon quickly burgeons into disgraceful alcoholism. At school, Richard fails to express any enthusiasm for knowledge, but later channels that enthusiasm into overexpression, proclaiming all his new, forbidden knowledge on the neighborhood windows. These behavioral swings demonstrate Richard's inability to interact with his family, friends, and society in a way consistent with their expectations. In response, his family, friends, and society punish him. In some ways, we can see this punishment by Richard's peers as similar to their lack of interest in engaging his curiosity about racism. Like curiosity, unpredictable behavior is a dangerous trait for a subordinate to show in a racist society.

Richard's acquisition of reading and counting skills are impressive intellectual feats. He accomplishes these feats with relative ease and speed, needing, for instance, only one hour to learn how to count to one hundred. More significant, Richard acquires these skills of his own free will—because he wants to, not because he is forced to. As such, Richard's feats of learning reveal his potential for powerful intelligence and intellectual curiosity, foreshadowing the quest for knowledge that will shape his life so decisively.

PART I: CHAPTER 2

SUMMARY

When Ella finally retrieves her children from the orphanage, Richard is so excited to leave that he only says goodbye to the other children because his mother demands it. In a brief digression from the story, Richard, as author, argues against the popular contention that black people lead particularly passionate, emotional lives. Rather, he believes that what others interpret as emotional depth in black people is really just frenzy and confusion occasioned by living as outsiders in America.

On the way to Elaine, Arkansas, where Ella's sister Maggie lives, Ella and her sons spend some time with Granny in Jackson, Mississippi. Granny is renting a room to a young schoolteacher, also named Ella. One day, Richard discovers the schoolteacher reading a book and implores her to tell him what the book is about. Hesitantly, Ella begins to describe the novel, *Bluebeard and His Seven Wives*. Richard is utterly enthralled by the fantasy world of the story, but Granny interrupts the reading before Ella can finish.

A strict Seventh-Day Adventist, Granny equates fiction with lies and sin, so she forbids such "Devil stuff" in her house. When Richard protests against his grandmother's restrictions, she slaps him and declares that he will burn in hell. Richard, however, is so enraptured by Ella's story that he becomes determined to read as many novels as he can, risk or no risk. He secretly borrows Ella's novels from her room and tries to read them, but cannot quite make sense of them because his vocabulary is too limited.

When Richard's mother falls ill, Granny assumes the task of bathing him and his brother. One particular night, while Granny is scrubbing his backside, Richard absentmindedly and uncomprehendingly tells her that when she is done she can kiss him "back there." Convinced that Richard is a mouthpiece for the Devil, Granny becomes enraged and begins beating him with a wet towel.

Richard flees. Upon learning of Richard's statement, his mother joins in the pursuit to punish him. Richard then crawls under a bed, where not even his grandfather can reach him. The boy remains there until hunger and thirst drive him out, at which point his mother beats him with a switch. To his mother's frustration, Richard is honestly unable to tell her where he learned the phrase he said. He is not even sure what the phrase means or why it constitutes such a grave insult. Granny, convinced that Richard has learned the phrase from Ella and her books, confronts the young schoolteacher, who decides to pack her things and move out.

Journeying to Aunt Maggie's in Arkansas, Richard notices separate sections on the train for white and black travelers. Out of naïve curiosity, Richard wants to go look at the white section, but his mother refuses and grows annoyed. He questions his mother about Granny's ancestry and race, which only annoys Ella further. Richard himself is annoyed that nobody will talk to him about race relations and resolves to learn whatever he can about this tricky issue.

Arriving in Arkansas, Richard discovers that Aunt Maggie and her husband, Hoskins, always have enough food, as Hoskins earns a good living from his profitable saloon. Nevertheless, Richard is so used to hunger that he hoards food all over the house, constantly fearing that the food will somehow run out. On a trip to a nearby town, Hoskins pulls a prank on Richard by jokingly driving the buggy into the Mississippi River. Though Hoskins knows the river is very shallow and safe, Richard is wildly fearful that they will be swept away and drowned. Unfortunately, Hoskins's joke makes Richard unable to trust his uncle. One night soon thereafter, local whites murder Hoskins because they covet his profitable business. Unable to claim Hoskins's body or his assets—and in danger of being murdered themselves—Ella, her two boys, and Maggie flee back to Granny's house.

One day, while playing at Granny's house, Richard sees a regiment of black soldiers training for World War I and, later, a black chain gang working by the roadside guarded by armed white men. In confusion, Richard thinks that the chain gang is a group of elephants, later realizing that the inmates' striped uniforms had reminded of him of zebras, which he had then confused with elephants. These sights cause Richard to once again ponder the mysterious division of power between white and black people.

Ella quickly tires of Granny's strict religious routine, so she, the two boys, and Aunt Maggie move out, resettling in West Helena,

Arkansas. While Maggie and Ella work, Richard and his brother entertain themselves by playing with other children and taunting the Jewish proprietor of the corner grocery store.

Richard learns that his landlady runs a curious business and resolves to learn more about it. He peeps over the door dividing his apartment from the neighboring one and sees a man and a woman having sex. Startled, Richard falls from his perch, causing the landlady to come over and scold him for scaring away her customers. The landlady then evicts Richard's family because his mother refuses to beat him as punishment for his nosiness.

Meanwhile, Maggie begins seeing an elegant man known only as Professor Matthews. Professor Matthews is hiding from the police, so he comes to see Maggie only at night and gives Richard and his brother gifts to ensure their silence. Among these gifts is a little female poodle that Richard names Betsy. After Professor Matthew commits a mysterious crime that seems to involve the death of a white woman, he and Maggie hurriedly flee to the North. Richard is sad to see them go because Maggie is his favorite aunt.

Without Maggie's income, the family once again falls into hard times. One day, Richard is so hungry that he resolves to sell Betsy for a dollar. He goes door-to-door in the white neighborhood and finds a white woman willing to buy the dog. Richard's mounting fear and hatred of white people, however, make him run home when the woman says that she has only ninety-seven cents on hand to pay for the dog. One week later, a coal wagon hits Betsy and kills her. Richard buries her mournfully, while Ella coldly reminds him that he should have sold Betsy when he had the chance, because a dead dog is useless.

As World War I draws to an end, racial tensions in the South rise. In hopeless confusion and fear, Richard listens to his neighbors' stories of violent racial conflict. A tale of a black woman's vengeance upon the white mob that killed her husband particularly impresses Richard, and he resolves to do something similar if he ever faces an angry mob.

Richard begins attending school again but suffers the same paralyzing shyness. One day, the war's end is suddenly announced, and the schoolteacher dismisses class early. Running outside, Richard sees a plane flying in the sky. It is the first time he has ever seen a plane, and he thinks it is a bird, refusing to believe the crowd's assertions that it is man-made. For Christmas that year, Richard receives only an orange.

ANALYSIS

In this section we see Richard develop an early love of literature that he likens to religious fervor. *Bluebeard and His Seven Wives*—the novel Ella the schoolteacher describes to Richard—is more a piece of pulp fiction than any literary masterpiece. However, in describing his reaction to the novel, Richard uses some surprisingly rich language, calling Ella's story "the first experience in my life that had elicited from me a total emotional response. . . . I had tasted what to me was life." We see Richard's deep emotional engagement, his punishment-defying certainty, and his life-affirming discovery that literature and writing are his calling. Richard's words here have an eloquent intensity that seems more suited to describing a religious experience than to describing a reaction upon learning the plot of a pulp novel. This unexpected seriousness places Richard's literary interests on an equal plane with religion.

Granny's clash with Ella and Richard over *Bluebeard* strengthens this idea that Richard's love of literature is akin to a religion. The violence of Granny's reaction suggests that, at some level, she believes that Richard's literary interests are a sincere threat to her faith—a faith that she desperately wants to rule over her household. For Richard, though, the distrust of art and human ingenuity that is inherent in Granny's faith prohibits true creativity. Granny demonstrates this distrust with her talk of "Devil stuff" and the irrational brutality with which she responds to Richard's desire to know the rest of the *Bluebeard* tale. In short, this scene poses Richard's educational interests as an alternative route to salvation. This conflict plays out in the rest of the novel, and we see that—on earth at least—Richard's way proves superior.

Wright's tale of Uncle Hoskins's river-crossing prank may not greatly affect Richard himself, but it has a great artistic effect on the novel. Though the prank terrifies Richard and makes him unable to trust his uncle, its effects end there. Richard says nothing about the prank's effects on the rest of his life, so we are led to assume that there are not any. From this biographical perspective, then, the river misadventure seems like a minor episode. However, the seemingly inexplicable prank and Richard's anxious reaction to it fill the chapter with a sense of unfathomable dread and evil— a sense of what English poet and critic Samuel Taylor Coleridge called "motiveless malignancy." Wright situates the prank scene in *Black Boy* so that it immediately precedes Hoskins's racially motivated murder. Racism, of course, is truly a "motiveless malignancy." As such, the prank scene foreshadows and underscores the murder's emotional dimensions, creating the ideal conditions into which it can erupt. From this artistic perspective, the river misadventure is significant and quite powerful—a masterful use of the form of autobiographical fiction.

The juxtaposition of the black soldiers with the black chain gang is an example of situational irony—circumstances that seem the opposite of what we might expect. On the one hand, Wright uses these images to imply that America must be a relatively black-friendly country if there are blacks who willingly volunteer to defend America in battle. When Richard sees the black soldiers, they are preparing to defend their country from "the enemy." Richard's mother defines the enemy as "people who want to kill you and take your country away from you," implying that the soldiers who lay down their lives in defense of their country must live in a very fine country. On the other hand, however, Wright uses the chain gang to demonstrate that black Americans receive unfairly harsh treatment from their country's justice system, suggesting that they do not in fact live in such a black-friendly land. When Richard sees the chain gang and wonders why so many black men are a part of it, his mother explains that white people are "harder on black people." These two facts—that black men will risk their lives to defend their country, yet that their country considers them second-class citizens—are difficult to reconcile. Because Wright links them so closely in the text, however, we are forced to try to reconcile them. All that emerges from this absurd attempt at reconciliation is irony.

PART I: CHAPTERS 3–4

SUMMARY: CHAPTER 3

> [T]he meaning of living came only when one was
> struggling to wring a meaning out of meaningless
> suffering.   (See QUOTATIONS, p. 71)

Richard becomes friends with the other black boys in his Arkansas neighborhood, finding that they share the same hostility to white people and the same racial pride. Wright remarks that he and the other boys did not entirely understand their motivations at the time. He reproduces one of their typical conversations along with a running commentary on the words the boys speak, which show that race is always the fundamental concern of the boys' interactions. The local black boys and white boys seem to assume their conventional racial roles "by instinct," meeting at the boundary of their respective territories for bloody battles fought with rocks, broken glass, pieces of iron, and anything else that can be thrown. In one fight, a broken bottle gives Richard a deep wound behind the ear that requires stitches. His mother takes him to the doctor for stitches but beats him when they get home, making him promise not to fight again. Richard feels he cannot honor his promise because these neighborhood fights are a matter of personal honor.

Ella becomes too ill to work, forcing her to move the family to a series of different apartments in an attempt to meet the rent payments. Richard works a variety of menial jobs to help with expenses. Ella suffers a paralytic stroke, and, though the neighbors assist in caring for his mother, Richard writes to Granny for help. The world around Richard, which heretofore had seemed somewhat harmless, suddenly appears bleak and hostile to him, and he begins to wonder what will happen if Granny doesn't come.

Though starving, Richard refuses the food offered by his neighbors, as he is ashamed to feel like an object of charity. When Granny arrives, Richard is glad that someone else will handle his mother's affairs, but he retains an understanding that he must now "face things alone." Richard helps the illiterate Granny by writing letters requesting money and support for Ella from her eight other children. Money from these aunts and uncles begins to arrive by mail. Ella, her sons, and Granny return to Granny's house in Jackson.

Back at Granny's house, Richard experiences terrible nightmares and fits of sleepwalking, which Granny treats by giving Richard more food and making him take naps in the afternoon. All of Richard's aunts and uncles come to Granny's house to help resolve the problem of how to care for Richard and his brother. The aunts and uncles decide to separate the two boys, as it would be too much of a burden for any one of them to care for both boys simultaneously. They decide to send Alan to live with his aunt Maggie in Detroit. To his surprise, Richard's aunts and uncles give him a choice of where he wants to live. He chooses to live with his uncle Clark in nearby Greenwood, Mississippi, so as to remain near his mother.

Richard feels nervous when Clark assigns him a long list of chores as soon as he arrives, but he feels better when he wakes up the next morning. That morning, Richard is mildly rebuked by Clark's wife, Aunt Jody, for failing to say good morning to her when he

SUMMARY & ANALYSIS

enters the kitchen. Richard then heads off to school, where he successfully fights another boy on the playground in order to gain acceptance from, and the respect of, his peers. That afternoon, Richard finds a ring in the street, removes the stone, and bends the ring's sharp prongs outward, making it into a weapon. He puts on the ring, expecting to have to fight again, but it proves unnecessary.

Just as Richard feels he is finally settling into his new life, he learns that the son of the previous occupant of Uncle Clark's house died in the bed that Richard now uses. Richard immediately grows terrified of the room and cannot sleep at all. Clark and Jody refuse to let him sleep on the sofa, and Richard's insomnia persists, bringing him to the edge of nervous exhaustion. Unable to endure the situation any longer, Richard asks to return to Granny's house. One day, while waiting for Granny's response to Clark's letter, Richard accidentally curses in front of Jody. After Clark punishes him with a beating, Richard begs so persistently to return to Jackson that Clark sends him right away.

Back at Granny's once again, Richard cannot wait to reach an age when he is old enough to support himself. His mother has much improved in his absence, but she suffers another paralytic stroke when she goes to nearby Clarksdale for an operation. Richard then knows that Ella has effectively left his life, as it seems clear that she will never be well again. Indeed, as Wright observes in retrospect, after her second stroke Ella remained bedridden for most of her remaining ten years. He then reflects that Ella's pain became a symbol to him for all the suffering and privation of his childhood and adolescent years. He writes that he came to believe, through his mother's suffering, that the meaning of life comes only from a struggle with meaningless pain.

SUMMARY: CHAPTER 4

Richard again faces hunger when he moves back to Jackson. His main meals are flour and lard mush for breakfast, followed by a plate of greens cooked in lard for dinner. He learns to temper his hunger, if only briefly, by drinking so much water that his stomach feels tight and full. Aunt Addie joins Granny in the fight to save Richard's soul, and tempers again flare.

Richard unwillingly enters the religious school where Addie teaches and finds the students there docile and boring. The tension between Richard and Addie escalates when she wrongly accuses Richard of eating walnuts in class. The guilty student was actually the one sitting directly in front of Richard, but Richard does not want to rat on his classmate. While trying to defend himself, Richard accidentally calls her "Aunt Addie" rather than "Miss Wilson," making her more furious. Addie beats Richard in front of the class, and he becomes furious that the guilty student has not come forward. Addie tells Richard that she is not yet through with him, but he resolves that she will not beat him again.

At home that evening, Richard tells Addie who the real culprit was, but she then decides to beat him again because he did not tell her this truth earlier in class. When she tries to do so, Richard grows frenzied and fends her off with a knife. He successfully defends himself, but Granny, Grandpa, and Ella all take Addie's side. They are more convinced than ever that something is seriously wrong with Richard. Wright then recalls that the only time he ever saw Addie laugh at school was when he was injured in a game of pop-the-whip that Addie had suggested the children play.

Religion attracts Richard emotionally, but on an intellectual level he is unable to believe in God. Granny forces Richard to attend certain all-night prayer meetings, but the twelve-year-old Richard's hormones make him more interested in the church elder's wife than in the elder's words.

A religious revival is coming through town, and Richard's family kindly urges him to attend, deciding that this is their last chance to reform him. Richard knows their true motives, however, and is unmoved. Granny recruits the neighborhood boys to try to convince Richard to go to God, but he can see his grandmother's workings behind his friends' words, and is not convinced. Richard is unable to explain to his peers his inability to believe in God. He has faith in the "common realities of life," not in any concept of cosmic order.

During a sermon one day at church, Richard whispers to Granny that he *would* believe in God if he saw an angel. Granny hears him incorrectly and thinks that he has said that he *has* seen an angel. She elatedly informs the church elder and the rest of the congregation. Richard, already mortified at Granny's misunderstanding, makes things worse by embarrassing her, correcting her error in front of everyone present at the church. Granny is furious.

To appease Granny's anger, Richard promises to pray every day, but he is unable to do so. The act of prayer even makes him laugh. To kill time during his daily prayer hour, he decides to write a story about an Indian maiden who drowns herself. In his excitement to share the story with someone, Richard reads it aloud to the young woman who lives next door. She seems astonished that anyone would write a story simply out of the desire to write, but Richard takes satisfaction from her puzzled bewilderment.

ANALYSIS: CHAPTERS 3–4

Wright's description of his interactions with the boys in Arkansas reveals the pain and futility he and these boys feel as black boys in a racist white society. The boys try to express defiance and seeming self-confidence through frequent anti-white declarations. However, as this defiance stems from the pain of constant oppression by whites, and because white oppression is far too massive for one person to stop alone, that air of confidence is fraught with insecurity. Wright indicates that the boys "frantically concealed how dependent we were upon one another." Like their parents' anxious conversations about race relations, the boys' fights accomplish nothing significant or lasting. Rather, they afford only the temporary emotional release gained by fighting over a boundary that will soon be violated once again. Though we see the boys' violent interracial fighting as pointless, we realize that the need to feel some sense of control, however fleeting, often expresses itself in irrational ways.

Richard's conflicts with Addie are intimately related to his problem with God and religion. Addie expects submission and meekness that, from Richard's perspective, goes beyond what she deserves. When she beats him in the classroom, he is very angry, but he can rationalize it to a degree because he knows that he appears guilty. At home, after Richard tells Addie who had really eaten the walnuts, she still wants to beat him, manufacturing the excuse that he was sinfully lying to her as a justification. But, as Richard's armed resistance demonstrates, the idea of abstract guilt does not strike a chord with him. Wright says that he has always had a notion of the suffering involved in life, but that it has never been tied to religion: "I simply could not feel weak and lost in a cosmic manner." He implies that the weakness that the concept of original sin—the idea of mankind's fundamental sinfulness, an essential doctrine of the Christian church—makes people feel is the only thing that makes them seek God. Thus, Wright's inability to feel fundamentally flawed and in need of correction makes him unable to submit not only to Addie, but to God as well. Rather, Wright feels lost in the sea change of his own life. The events of these chapters give dramatic testimony to the unpredictability of Richard's life, making it easy for us to understand Richard's difficulty in believing in any doctrine of cosmic order.

For Wright, the meaning of life lies in the very act of striving to find the meaning of life. This idea is essential to existentialism, a school of twentieth-century philosophical thought to which Wright ascribed later in his life. Existentialism asserts that many of the most important choices we need to make in life—such as whether to believe in God or whether to believe in love—have no rational or objective basis. Such notions of rationality and objectivity are merely the inventions of humankind. The only thing that humans can ever know is that which they can observe directly. Existentialist thought also holds that we can make life meaningful through individual creativity and through the active acceptance of our own self-created values. In *Black Boy,* Wright claims that "no education could ever alter" his conclusion that the meaning of life is discernible "only when one [is] struggling to wring a meaning out of meaningless suffering." Wright wrote *Black Boy* during 1943–1944, but came into contact with existentialism late in 1947, when he moved to Paris. After meeting two of its major proponents, Jean-Paul Sartre and Simone de Beauvoir, Wright came to embrace existentialism. He did so not because it was fashionable—although, at the time, it was very fashionable indeed—but because it resonated with beliefs he had always held.

PART I: CHAPTER 5

SUMMARY

Granny and Addie decide that Richard is lost to the world and finally give up the effort to save his soul. This means that the two women grow cold and hostile toward him, but it also means that he can leave Addie's religious school for a public school. Granny refuses to pay for Richard's public school textbooks because she considers them worldly.

On the first day of school, Richard fights two boys simultaneously after one of them knocks his straw hat off his head. As usual, he proves himself and gains acceptance through fighting. Within two weeks, Richard advances from the fifth grade to the sixth. Richard is unable to find a job that does not require him to work on Saturday, a day Granny refuses to allow him to work for religious reasons. Richard's lack of income prevents him from participating in the social life of his classmates, which revolves around buying snacks at the corner store. He hides his poverty from his peers, all the while yearning to be a part of their group, wanting to eat with them and to get to know them intimately.

A classmate tells Richard that he sells newspapers to make money and suggests that Richard do the same. The classmate has never read the Chicago-printed paper itself, but he likes the stories in the magazine supplement that comes with it. Richard orders a batch of the papers and becomes entranced by the stories his friend has told him about. He makes some money selling these papers for a while, as Granny has permitted him the job because it does not require him to sell on Saturdays.

One day, one of Richard's black customers takes him aside and asks him if he really is aware of what he is selling. He shows Richard that the paper, which Richard still has never read, is filled with propaganda from the Ku Klux Klan, the vicious white supremacist group. Richard is shocked, knowing that the paper is printed in Chicago, a place, he has heard, where blacks are supposedly equal to whites. Richard immediately stops selling the paper. When the father of Richard's classmate discovers the content of the paper, he forbids his son to sell it as well. Out of mutual shame, Richard and his classmate never discuss why they stopped selling the paper. Without money from his job, Richard goes hungry yet again.

One day, while Addie and Granny endlessly debate details of religious doctrine, Richard makes an offhand comment that the women deem blasphemous. Granny vigorously lunges to slap Richard, but he ducks the blow, and Granny loses her balance, falling off the porch and injuring her back. Later, Richard wants to ask how Granny is doing, but he cannot let his guard down in front of Addie. Addie confronts him in the hallway and tries to beat him. Once again, Richard fends off the blows, crying hysterically and brandishing a knife from the kitchen. Addie vows that she will give him his due beating one night. Consequently, Richard sleeps with a knife under his pillow for the next month. Wright makes the observation that these constant religious disputes made his family's household even more quarrelsome and violent than the household of a gangster or burglar.

Richard then takes a job writing for Brother Mance, an illiterate insurance salesman who lives next door. The job entails journeys to plantations, which prove to be eye-opening experiences for Richard, who is alarmed to see the universal poverty, isolation, and ignorance of Southern black sharecroppers. Richard notes the consistently shy nature of the sharecroppers' children; compared to them, he feels like a civilized man from the big city.

One morning, Richard learns that Grandpa is seriously ill. A Union veteran of the Civil War, Grandpa has been deprived of his pension due to a simple clerical error in his benefits application. One rumor has it that a white Southern officer deliberately made this error to deprive Grandpa of his due. Grandpa has tried to claim his pension for decades, but the War Department never accepts the evidence he submits to prove that he did in fact fight in the Civil War. Eternally bitter at this injustice, Grandpa has remained cold and distant to everyone, including Richard.

When Grandpa dies, the family sends Richard to report the news to his uncle Tom, who now lives nearby. Richard wakes Tom and immediately blurts out that Grandpa has died. Tom takes offense at the indelicate way Richard reports his father's death, causing Richard to wonder why he never seems to be able to please other people. Richard is not invited to the funeral.

Eventually, Richard's clothes grow so shabby that he is embarrassed to wear them to school. He forces Granny to let him work on Saturdays by threatening to move out, calling her bluff. Granny and Addie make it clear that Richard is now truly dead to them. Richard's mother, however, is proud of him for defying them.

ANALYSIS

In his move to the public school, Richard displays his trademark determination to go his own way against all odds. Public school requires Richard to spend his own money, as Granny forbids him from any job that entails Saturday work—effectively barring him from all employment—and he must pay for the public school textbooks out of his own pocket. Therefore, Richard's desire to leave Addie's religious school puts him in a dilemma, as leaving would be satisfying but would mean mounting costs with little means to pay them, while staying would be unsatisfying but would ensure him some degree of financial support for his education. The price of remaining subject to Addie's scorn and fury, however, is too much for Richard's character to bear. The problem of paying his way in pubic school has no easy solution, but Richard—feeling like he has been "released from a prison"—is overjoyed to embrace that problem.

Richard's unwitting distribution of the Klan newspaper is mean-ingful both in the context of his own life story and in the context of broader black American culture. At a most basic level, it reveals Richard's naïveté in his belief that racism could never flourish in the North. In this sense, the incident with the paper foreshadows similar surprises Richard experiences when he eventually makes the move North himself. More broadly, we can also see the incident with the paper as a criticism Wright directs at the black American commu-nity in general. The man who shows Richard the error of his ways does so gently, but does not shy away from using stern language: "you're just helping white people to kill you." Wright implies that he should have known better and should not have been so ignorant. By extension, Wright is warning the black community that they will end up working against their own causes if they fail to educate them-selves about the world around them. Wright readily admits that as a youth he was guilty of this error himself.

Richard's travels with the insurance salesman make his life look rich in comparison to the lives of the sharecroppers. The poverty and illiteracy that mar the lives of blacks on the plantations demon-strate that Richard's literacy and worldly wisdom—the wisdom gained by moving so frequently from place to place—are real, if hard-won, blessings. However, when we consider the painful, glar-ing poverty Richard endures, we realize how truly terrible the con-ditions of the sharecroppers' existence must be. In this way, Richard's travels with the insurance man provide an interesting context for thinking about what might have happened to Richard. After all, Richard himself is the son of a sharecropper and could eas-ily have turned out just like the people he visits.

Grandpa's endless battle with the War Department raises ethical questions about the American government. Although we do not actually see the letters that Grandpa receives after submitting his pension claim, we assume that they use official- and objective-sounding language to assert that Grandpa's claims are unsubstanti-ated and must be rejected. Wright's reference to the rumor that a white Southern officer deliberately misspelled Grandpa's name, however, adds a sinister aspect to the government action, casting doubt on the supposedly objective nature of its official business. Wright strengthens that doubt by dwelling on Grandpa's illiteracy, as we realize that bureaucracy and paperwork make it especially easy for the government to take advantage of illiterate people. Wright implies that Grandpa's bureaucratic troubles might be explained, at least in part, by the fact that he is black, illiterate, and therefore vulnerable to attack in America.

PART I: CHAPTERS 6–8

SUMMARY: CHAPTER 6

Richard interviews for a job working in the home of a white family, and his prospective employer asks him outright if he will steal from her. Richard laughs and tells the woman that if he were going to steal from her, he definitely would not tell her. The woman is angered but gives him the job anyway, which pays modestly but includes meals. Richard ends up disliking the job, however, because though the white family eats plentifully, the woman offers Richard only moldy food to eat. Moreover, when the woman asks Richard why he still bothers to attend school and he replies that he wants to be a writer, she rudely mocks him. He quits almost immediately.

Richard's next job, with another white family, is equally unpleasant. The family members are phenomenally rude and ungrateful both to each other and to him. Richard keeps the job nonetheless, because he is able to steal a considerable amount of food from the family on the side. Though the emotional stress of the job strains him, it enables him to become a full member of the community of his peers. Armed with wages and brimming with tales about his white employers, Richard can now eat lunch with his classmates and swap stories.

Ella's health improves, and Richard begins attending a Methodist church with her. The church holds a religious revival in which the preacher calls for mothers to persuade their wayward sons to accept God. Singled out by the preacher, Richard and the several other unbelieving youths feel such pressure from the congregation that they allow themselves to be baptized even though they do not truly believe in God. After the baptism, Richard admits to the other baptized boys that he does not feel any different, and they voice similar sentiments.

Soon thereafter, Ella suffers yet another paralytic stroke. Money is running tight, so Granny allows Uncle Tom and his family to move in, in exchange for a small rent. One morning, Tom awakens Richard to ask him what time it is. When Richard tells him the time, his uncle does not believe that it is accurate, but Richard checks again and offhandedly says that the time he had given was close enough. Tom gets incredibly angry and vows to give Richard the whipping of his life for what he perceives as unfathomable insubordination. Richard fights Tom off with two razors, shocking his uncle and breaking his domineering spirit.

SUMMARY: CHAPTER 7

During the summer before eighth grade, Richard works as a water boy and brick gatherer in the local brickyard. One afternoon the boss's dog bites Richard, which worries him because he knows that several other workers have fallen ill after being bitten by the dog. Richard meets with the boss, but he does not take Richard seriously, claiming, "A dog bite can't hurt a nigger." Fortunately, though the wound gets inflamed, it heals on its own in a few days.

Richard starts the eighth grade, depressed that his education has furnished him with no skills to help him earn a living. Though he dwells on racism and can only think of it in terms of the large-scale, universal injustice it represents, his classmates limit their discussion of racism to individual, personal wrongs they have experienced.

Richard writes a short story called "The Voodoo of Hell's Half-Acre" and persuades the local black paper to print it. His classmates cannot understand why he has written and published a story simply because he wanted to do so. Richard's family is likewise unreceptive and hostile—Granny and Addie equate literary fiction with lies, while Ella thinks that Richard's writing will lead people to think he has a weak mind and thus will not want to hire him. The newspaper editor is literally the only person who encourages him. Wright muses that if he had known then how many obstacles he would eventually have to overcome to become a writer, he would have abandoned his quest.

SUMMARY: CHAPTER 8

The following summer, Richard looks for a job at the local sawmill, but leaves after one of the workers demonstrates the danger of sawmill work by showing Richard his right hand, which is missing three fingers. One morning Richard learns that whites have killed the brother of one of his black classmates because they thought he was consorting with a white prostitute in a local hotel where he worked. The killing burdens Richard's consciousness even further with the grim reality and pervasiveness of white oppression.

Richard learns that Uncle Tom thinks his nephew is such a bad influence on his children that he has instructed his children to avoid

Richard around the house. This realization makes Richard's longing for independence stronger than ever. Alan, Richard's brother, soon visits the family, and much to Richard's dismay his brother quickly adopts the family's critical attitude toward him.

Richard is named valedictorian of his class, but he discovers that the principal will not let him give his own speech at the ceremony. Because white people will be present at the graduation, the principal has written a speech of his own, which he instructs Richard to deliver. The principal threatens to keep Richard from graduating if he insists on giving a different speech. Richard's family, friends, and classmates all urge him to avoid trouble and just deliver the principal's speech, but he adamantly refuses.

When the day of graduation arrives, Richard gives his own speech and immediately flees the auditorium, paying no attention to the applause, to the handshakes, to the invitations to parties that he receives. He is disgusted with the community, the event, and with the fact that he lived his life for seventeen years in a baffled state. Wright muses that at this point he finally resolved to put this baffled living behind him and "faced the world in 1925."

ANALYSIS: CHAPTERS 6–8

However sassy Uncle Tom may regard Richard's comments on the accuracy of the clock to be, the violence of Tom's reaction far exceeds rational bounds and is difficult to comprehend. We might think that Richard should expect this sort of behavior from adult men, given that he has a history of traumatic relationships with nearly every man in his family. The examples are numerous: Richard's sullen and prickly grandfather, his uncle Hoskins's disastrous river-crossing prank, his father's alarmingly remorseless abandonment of the family, the fear of a dead boy's ghost that pervades his uncle Clark's house, and the close association of his pseudo-uncle the "Professor"—with whom Maggie goes north—with the murder of a white person. Adding to this problematic series of male family relationships is the fact that the women in Richard's life are all either ill or fanatically religious. It is understandable, then, that Richard feels so withdrawn and isolated. In this light, it seems extremely fortunate that his spirit is strong enough to champion such independence and adhere to the standards that guide his actions.

Wright's commentary on his dream of becoming a writer indicates the devastating reality of growing up black in the Jim Crow

South. The reaction of Richard's white boss upon learning that Richard wants to be a writer is predictable—vulgar, brutal, and contemptuous. Obviously, Richard can expect no support from the white community. The black community, however, is practically as unsupportive of Richard's writing as the white community. Indeed, the black community's reaction to the publication of Richard's story is shocking: his friends are uncomprehending, and his family, with the exception of his concerned mother, is scornful.

This parallel between the white and black communities' reactions to Richard's aspirations reveals the degree to which the black imagination is oppressed in Richard's culture. In one sense, *Black Boy* clearly stands as an indictment of racism in America and its negative effect on blacks. At the same time, however, it is an attempt on Wright's part to criticize the black community itself for succumbing to the pressures of racism and allowing them to negatively influence their relations with one another. Of course, many black Americans in the South did derive benefits from their community, drawing positive strength from unifying forces such as religion. However, as Wright experienced particularly bad luck by being born into an abusive family that could not tolerate his individuality, he can highlight only the disastrous limitations of growing up in the South. Though only one perspective, Wright's voice is nonetheless very important, and his point that the oppressed cannot afford to victimize themselves in the face of racism is powerful and salient.

While Richard's actions at his graduation ceremony may seem like a satisfying moral victory, his disgust implies that it is merely the beginning of an adult life marked by more hardship, social exclusion, and dismal labor. Richard's negative reaction after the ceremony is complicated but understandable. At first, it is not immediately clear why Richard feels disgust: being named valedictorian is quite an honor in itself, and in addition Richard has given his own speech, triumphing over those who had wanted him to compromise his standards and deliver the principal's speech instead. Despite these seeming triumphs, Richard is nonetheless discouraged because the triumphs do not outweigh the discouraging facts of his life. Though continuing in the educational system—either as a teacher or as a higher-level student—would appear to be Richard's best hope for advancement, the principal's actions reveal how thoroughly corrupt this educational system is. Richard's core values lead him to defy that corruption, but this defiance earns him only criticism from his community. Finally, with his education bound to end at the ninth grade, Richard knows that the only future jobs he can expect are degrading ones, just like the ones he has already had.

In retrospect, however, Wright indicates that his actions at graduation may have had some positive effects on the community. Though at the time he focused only on the negative aspects of the event, looking back he mentions that some people clapped, tried to shake his hand, and invited him to parties. Indeed, the audience did not shun him; rather, he shunned the audience. Richard's response seems melodramatic, and we sense that at least part of Wright's isolation as a youth may stem from such self-isolating actions that he initiates himself. Though his home life and social life are indeed undeniably difficult, Richard's stubborn personality is another factor that hinders his growth.

PART I: CHAPTERS 9–11

SUMMARY: CHAPTER 9

Richard takes a job at a clothing store where the white bosses humiliate the black customers on a daily basis. Richard sees the shopkeepers beat a black woman who is unable to pay the credit installments on her clothing purchase. One day, Richard's bicycle gets a flat tire after he makes a clothing delivery. A group of young white men offer to let him ride back to town on the side of their car. When Richard neglects to call one of the white youths "sir," they smash a whiskey bottle in his face, causing him to fall from the speeding vehicle. He walks back to town.

Not long thereafter, when Richard makes a delivery in a white neighborhood, suspicious policemen force him to the side of the road and aggressively search him at gunpoint. They tell Richard to tell his boss not to send him on delivery runs in white neighborhoods after dark. Eventually, Richard's boss fires him because he does not like Richard's silent disapproval of the way he runs the store and treats black people.

Griggs, a former classmate, admonishes Richard for not knowing how to act around white people. He tells Richard that his reputation as a troublemaker has already been spread to many potential white employers. After repeatedly stressing that Richard must swallow his pride and learn to feign humility in order to survive around whites, Griggs helps Richard secure a job with Mr.

Crane, a Northerner interested in training a black boy in the trade of optics and lens-making.

Richard is elated and eagerly reports to Crane's optical shop. However, Richard's white coworkers, Pease and Reynolds, refuse to teach him how to work the machines, asserting that it is "white man's work." They belittle Richard with crude questions about his anatomy and constantly attempt to intimidate him. One day, Pease says that Reynolds has told him that Richard once referred to him as simply "Pease" rather than the more respectful "Mr. Pease." Richard knows he is in a trap: if he admits to this charge, Pease will punish him for disrespect, but if he denies the charge, Reynolds will punish Richard for implying that he is a liar. Richard knows that the men are trying to drive him out of the shop, so he quits.

Richard feels totally demoralized. The sympathetic Crane calls Richard into his office and asks him what happened, but Richard refuses to tell, out of fear that Reynolds and Pease will gather a mob and kill him. Crane then pays Richard more than he has earned for the week, apologizes for being unable to do more, and tells Richard he approves of Richard's plan to move to the North. Crane says he understands that blacks lead a hard life in the South, and believes that a move to the North is perhaps Richard's best hope. Richard feels terribly violated and ashamed. He thanks Crane hastily and leaves, in his own words, as "a blind man."

SUMMARY: CHAPTER 10

Richard drifts from job to job, so exhausted and dispirited by the constant threat of racism that he frequently makes mistakes that get him fired. When the summer ends and many of the other boys return to school, jobs become plentiful. Richard takes a job at the same hotel where his classmate's brother had worked until he was murdered for consorting with a white prostitute. At the hotel, Richard mops hallways with a group of young black men, including one who amuses Richard because he takes pride in having gonorrhea, which he claims is a mark of manhood. One day, a white security guard fondles one of the black maids, and Richard's obvious displeasure leads the guard to threaten him with a gun.

Richard hesitates to engage in the thievery rampant among the hotel workers because he does not consider it worth the risk of being caught. He acknowledges, however, that racism encourages such theft, as whites would rather have a dishonest, uneducated black worker than an honest, educated one.

Eventually, Richard changes his mind and decides to steal so that he can raise money to move North, reasoning that living honestly would merely prolong his stay in the South. He leaves his job at the hotel and takes one at a movie theater, where he helps his coworkers steal two hundred dollars by reselling tickets. Burning to leave the South, he steals a gun from a neighbor and pawns it for money. He then resells some fruit preserves that he has stolen from a nearby black college. With this money, Richard goes to Memphis. His stealing pains him, and he vows never to do it again.

SUMMARY: CHAPTER 11

In Memphis, Richard rents a room from a black woman named Mrs. Moss. She delights Richard with her kindness and generosity. It immediately becomes clear that, although she has just met him, she wants him to marry her daughter, Bess. Unaccustomed to trusting people, Richard feels stunned and slightly disgusted that Mrs. Moss can so wholeheartedly accept and trust someone she barely knows. Moreover, Bess is not attractive to him; he finds her childish and dull.

The next morning, Richard meets another young black man while sitting on the waterfront. They find some bootleg liquor hidden in a patch of weeds and decide to sell it. A white man says he will give them five dollars for the liquor if they will move it to his car. Richard feels uneasy, but the young black man appears more than willing, and Richard assists. The black man leaves Richard to get change for the five-dollar bill so they can split it, but he does not come back. Richard is annoyed with himself for not realizing that the black man and the white man had been working together and had used Richard to help them move the illegal liquor.

ANALYSIS: CHAPTERS 9–11

Richard's inability to meet his family's expectations throughout the early parts of *Black Boy* foreshadows the inability to show humility before—and thus avoid confrontations with—the whites that he displays in these chapters. The fundamental source of Richard's difficulties with his family is his inability to obey their orders: he can never submit to his family's demands that he humble himself to their authority, so he receives violent beatings as punishment. Here, we see that Richard has similar trouble hiding his pride and judgment in the presence of whites, which results in similar negative consequences. To paraphrase his friend Griggs, Richard's problem is that when he is around whites he acts as if he does not notice that they are white. He does not bend over backward to humble himself as whites expect him to, and, consequently, he reaps violence. The burst of violent racism in Chapter 9 may startle us, but it fits with the already established pattern of Richard's family life.

Mr. Crane symbolizes how even well-meaning whites commit subtle acts of racism. At first glance, Crane appears sensitive toward Richard, and when push comes to shove he shows compassion, asking Richard genuine questions about how he was terrorized, giving him more money than he is due, and repeatedly saying that he is sorry about the whole situation. The fact that Pease and Reynolds can only terrorize Richard when Crane is out of the office implies that Crane would defend Richard. At the same time, however, Crane shows signs of the typical white superiority complex in relation to Richard. He makes Richard wait a full half-hour before speaking with him just because he wants to peruse the mail. He also shows his lack of understanding by remarking that life in the South is tough not just for Richard but for himself as well. Though Crane may indeed have a rough time controlling the racial turmoil in his factory, and may face some criticism from fellow whites for his sympathy toward blacks, his troubles cannot begin to compare with Richard's problems. Crane is unable to do anything to help Richard beyond apologizing and giving him some extra cash. While these are undeniably kind gestures, they merely attempt to compensate Richard for enduring racism instead of trying to redress the racism itself.

It is somewhat difficult to judge the extent of Crane's genuine sympathy toward Richard because Wright does not comment on it. We can only assume Wright does not comment on Crane's attitude because he wants us to think for ourselves about how racism—or rather our conceptions of racism—make it difficult to form a definite impression of others' intentions. Racism is a difficult problem not just because of its overt violence and discrimination, but because it often operates in much more subtle forms. Mr. Crane clearly shows Richard some degree of kindness, but something nonetheless prevents him from treating Richard as an equal.

Chapter 11 is a chapter of reversals. In the overall context of *Black Boy*, the move to the city itself represents a reversal. Richard's agonizing small-town life is quickly replaced by a surprisingly comfortable life in the city. In the process, he exchanges despair for hope and antagonistic relationships for easy and trustful ones. Likewise, another reversal occurs when Bess shifts from passionately declaring her love for Richard to passionately declaring her hatred for him. Moreover, Richard does not believe he merits Mrs. Moss's and Bess's trust because he is hustling them, but then he himself is hustled when the white and black strangers team up and use him to unload the bootleg liquor. Wright presents these last two events in such away that they achieve a meaningful symmetry—Richard's "hustling" of Bess and her mother is balanced by his being hustled the next day. At the center of all of these changes lies the city, a setting Wright presents as a highly dynamic place, where tremendous changes and shifts occur in short spans of time.

PART I: CHAPTERS 12–14

SUMMARY: CHAPTER 12

Richard takes a job in another optical shop, where he cleans and runs errands. The black elevator man, Shorty, amuses Richard, as he is clearly sensible and intelligent but nonetheless totally willing to demean himself for money. Several times Richard witnesses Shorty allowing a white man to kick him for a quarter. A Northern white customer notices Richard's thin frame and tries to offer him money to buy food, but Richard is too ashamed to accept it. Meanwhile, Bess and Mrs. Moss have finally come to understand that Richard has no interest in joining their family.

To amuse themselves, Richard's foreman, Olin, and the white employees of a competing optical shop try to instigate a fight between Richard and Harrison, the black employee in the other shop. They tell each man that the other is planning to kill him. Richard and Harrison meet secretly and figure out what is going on, but they still remain suspicious of one another. The white men offer to pay Richard and Harrison five dollars each to box one another. They agree, planning to fake the fight. When the fight starts, however, Richard and Harrison realize that they do not know how to fake it. Their frustrations at being manipulated take over, and they fight each other genuinely and viciously.

SUMMARY: CHAPTER 13

> *I concluded the book with the conviction that I had*
> *somehow overlooked something terribly important in*
> *life.* (See QUOTATIONS, p. 72)

Richard reads an editorial in a Memphis newspaper that attacks H.L. Mencken, the essayist and critic. Intrigued that a Southern newspaper would attack a white man, Richard resolves to read some of Mencken's work. As blacks are not permitted to borrow books from the public library, Richard asks a white Irish Catholic coworker, Falk, if he can use Falk's library card to check out books. Falk agrees but urges Richard to be careful.

Richard forges a note from Falk to the librarian, asking that she give "this nigger boy" some Mencken books for him. The librarian is momentarily suspicious but gives Richard the books. Mencken's boldness and verbal swordplay inspire Richard to become a voracious reader. The books bring him an exciting new understanding of life, and he hungers to do some writing of his own. Richard cautiously hides his books from his coworkers, who notice that he has become distant and dreamy. That winter, Richard's mother and brother join him in Memphis. Alan gets a job, and the family anxiously saves money for the trip to Chicago.

SUMMARY: CHAPTER 14

Soon after Richard's mother and brother arrive, Maggie moves to Memphis because her husband, Matthews—the mysterious "Professor"—has abandoned her. Desiring to reach Chicago as quickly as possible, everyone decides that Richard and Maggie will go first and get a place for the four of them. The other two will follow once they have enough money.

Southern whites do not like it when black people move to the North because it implies that the blacks do not like the treatment they receive in the South. To minimize this friction, Richard waits until only two days before his departure to tell his boss that he is leaving. Moreover, in order to minimize the appearance that he actively wants to leave the South, Richard says that he is leaving only to be near his mother. Richard's white coworkers at the optical shop appear bewildered by the news and become slightly resentful. Falk, however, gives him a sly smile. Shorty is jealous that Richard is leaving and bids him a bittersweet farewell, lamenting that his own laziness will likely prevent him from following Richard's lead.

ANALYSIS: CHAPTERS 12–14

Richard's interactions with Harrison show that the burden of racism sometimes prevents the oppressed from acting rationally or humanely. When the two of them meet, they establish that neither wants to kill, or even fight, the other. This reconciliation should neutralize any tension between them, but Richard realizes that considerable suspicion remains. Similarly, their boxing match makes little sense from a rational perspective, as both Richard and Harrison understand that they are no threat to each other. To help us understand this odd situation, Wright emphasizes how Richard and Harrison are unable to escape the emotional pressures of racism enough to truly care about the other man. Olin's rumors about the impending threat of murder infect Richard and Harrison to such an extent that they remain suspicious of one another. Moreover, during the actual fight, Richard and Harrison, wanting to avoid an angry white response, are anxious to show that they believe the rumors on some level. As Richard's society punishes black insubordination with severe violence, or even death, the powerful instinct to stay alive and avoid harm compels blacks to do anything possible to avoid the appearance of insubordination. Richard and Harrison hate themselves for being so easily manipulated, but the violence inherent in racism precludes them from acting on their humane impulses. Racism and violence simply breed more violence.

The transformation of Richard's outlook through his reading of H. L. Mencken resonates in numerous similar transformations in other texts, including autobiographies by other African-American writers. In *I Know Why the Caged Bird Sings,* Maya Angelou describes her fascination with literature, poetry, and drama. Literature serves as her inspirational escape from the evils of the racist and hateful society in which she lives. Though she sometimes isolates herself from the world by spending hours at the library, the positive effects of reading ultimately outweigh the negative effects of isolation. Literature abounds with other such examples of people not only enraptured by what they read, but transformed so deeply that the world seems a richer, more stimulating place. When Wright says that he "concluded [reading] the book with the conviction that I had somehow overlooked something terribly important in life," he links his story to this tradition of transformative readings. At the same time, however, Wright's statement also highlights the fact that *Black Boy* stands out as a critique of the African-American family and its folk traditions. Wright looks back on his childhood with regret, and only fully realizes the importance of literature in his life at the end of his autobiography. Angelou, in contrast, does not show regret for her exposure to folk traditions, and though she does not overlook the negative aspects of black life, she primarily focuses on its positives.

Wright also implies that hateful cultures often contain the seeds of their own undoing. Though he focuses primarily on the prejudice whites show toward blacks, he does not ignore the other forms of prejudice that he encounters in his youth. One such prejudice is anti-Catholicism. Catholic-Protestant hostility dates back centuries, and many people in the predominantly Protestant South regard Catholics with suspicion. Richard hears the other white men refer to Falk as a "Pope lover"—an insult against the Catholic faith. As Richard is likewise the butt of such contemptuous language, he feels a sort of solidarity with Falk. This fraternal feeling leads Richard to reason that Falk may be willing to help him. Luckily, in this case Richard is correct, and the help he receives from Falk not only illuminates the complex system of prejudices in Richard's world, but also suggests a way to challenge these prejudices. Out of a shared sense of injustice, the groups excluded by the majority culture form relationships and find ways to circumvent the rules that restrain them. We see Richard applying this notion of using certain aspects of racism to one's own advantage when he includes the word "nigger" in his forged note to the librarian. Richard inverts a term that is normally used to abuse him in order to get what he wants. Wright seems to approve of exploiting these racist elements as an effective means of resisting common oppression.

The fact that Southern whites fear and discourage black migration to the North exposes the degree to which their pride—and even their very economic welfare—depends on the presence of blacks. Racism is a means to an end, as oppressors employ racist measures in order to achieve power over another group. Wright shows numerous times throughout the novel that racism breeds irrational actions, times when Southern whites abuse blacks for no reason other than to vent their own frustration. This abuse and subordination of blacks also serves an economic function for the whites, as the blacks are the menial laborers who almost single-handedly support the white economy, for meager pay. Whites abuse blacks in order to keep them in a position where their service would empower whites. Therefore, Wright provides a sort of dismally humorous lesson in the reactions of Richard's white coworkers when they learn he is moving to Chicago. Their stupid and sour comments plainly reveal the frustration they feel that Richard is escaping his punishing existence for a freer one in the North.

PART II
(THE HORROR AND THE GLORY):
CHAPTER 15

SUMMARY

> *Our too-young and too-new America . . . insists upon seeing the world in terms of good and bad, the holy and the evil, the high and the low, the white and the black. . . . Am I damning my native land? No; for I, too, share these faults of character!*

(See QUOTATIONS, p. 73)

Richard arrives in Chicago and finds the city startling. The city's bleak industrial landscape depresses him and fills him with fears for his success. The casual interactions between blacks and whites bewilder him. He gets a room in the building where his aunt Cleo lives. He goes looking for a job the next morning, and finds one as a porter in a delicatessen owned by the Hoffmans, an immigrant Jewish couple. The work is easy, but Richard has a great deal of trouble understanding the Hoffmanses' thick accents. Richard wrongly assumes that their occasional impatience with him stems from racism.

Richard muses on the dehumanizing social status of black Americans. He notices that the Hoffmans own and operate their store in a whites-only neighborhood. Tortured by the perpetual uncertainty of his fate, Wright discusses his constant fear that he will inadvertently offend the whites who tolerate his presence in the neighborhood. This fear brings Richard closer to sympathizing with other black people who appear to surrender to racism—people like Shorty. Richard does not approve of such surrender, but he now understands why it occurs.

Chicago inspires in Richard new dreams and desires, but he wonders which, if any, can come true. Rather than focusing on "external events" like lynchings, Richard comes to understand that being black in America is a life of constant "psyche pain," not merely physical pain. He thinks that few blacks can fully comprehend or tell the story of their pain.

Richard takes an examination to be a postal clerk. Out of fear that the Hoffmans will fire him if he dares to look at another job, he simply stays away from work for three days while he rests and takes the examination. When he returns, he explains his absence with the lie that his mother died in Memphis and that he had to go the funeral. The Hoffmans tell him they know he is lying, but they let him stay because they like him. They insist that they are not like Southerners. Richard is ashamed that he has lied out of fear, but he still cannot admit his lie. He quits his job the following Saturday, without telling the Hoffmans anything, because he is too ashamed to work there any longer.

Richard gets a job as a dishwasher in a café. His white female coworkers seem ignorant, careless, and shallow, but pleasant enough. They occasionally brush against him as they maneuver around the restaurant, which stuns him, because a black man touching a white woman, even inadvertently, is a dreadful offense in the South.

Richard's white female boss is amused when she finds him reading the *American Mercury*—the magazine H. L. Mencken edits. Richard is horrified to discover that Tillie, the Finnish cook, spits in the food, and he tells a black girl, recently hired as a salad chef, about it. Richard and the girl want to tell the boss, but they wonder if she will believe them in light of the fact that they are black. The girl finally decides to tell the boss, and Richard confirms her testimony. The boss observes Tillie spitting and fires her immediately.

Meanwhile, Richard takes a temporary job with the post office. The work is ideal, as it pays well and affords him time to write. However, he must meet a weight requirement of 125 pounds in order to obtain a permanent appointment, but he currently barely weighs 110. Richard eats and sleeps heartily, but he gains no weight and fails the physical examination for the job.

Richard has no friends but does not feel the need for any. His mother and brother have arrived, and he shares an apartment with them and Maggie. His voracious reading still puzzles his family, and they think he is wasting his time with books. Richard's attempts at writing frustrate him, as he is unable to match the high quality of the novels he reads. Having failed the weight requirement, Richard needs a new job and resumes his job at the café. He learns that another postal examination is scheduled for spring. Determined to make weight, he begins forcing food down, eating to the point of feeling ill. Meanwhile, he reads Proust's *A Remembrance of Things Past* and despairs that he will never be able to write so eloquently about his own experiences.

ANALYSIS

Just as Richard's journey from the countryside to Memphis marks a great series of reversals for Richard, the move from Memphis to Chicago forces him to make numerous revisions in his outlook on the world. Richard's difficulty interacting with the Hoffmans indicates that he needs to revise his attitudes toward white people. He has come to Chicago ascribing to the Southern code of relations with whites, and he attempts to cling to this code despite its inappropriateness in the North. Richard's strategy for taking time off for the postal examination—to take the time without asking and then later make up lies to justify it—would have been appropriate in the South, where the relationship between blacks and whites is, in Wright's word, "paternalistic." However, as the relationship between blacks and whites is different in Chicago, Richard's strategy fails. Though the Hoffmans are white, they are kind, calm people genuinely interested in Richard—a far cry from the whites he grew up obeying and fearing. Admittedly, Crane showed Richard some degree of care, attention, and respect, but his motives do not seem as genuine as the those of the Hoffmans. We sympathize with Richard's uneasiness around the Hoffmans, but we are aware that he will need to overcome this instinct if he ever wants to trust white people in the future.

The episode with Tillie, in addition to being thrillingly nasty, represents an important step in the development of Richard's new relationship with whites. The episode would have played out very differently in the South: Richard would never have informed on a white coworker for fear of violence, and even if he had, a white boss would likely have dismissed Richard's testimony solely because of his race. These thoughts are clearly on Richard's mind after he sees Tillie spit, as he does not tell his boss right away. When he and his coworker finally do tell on Tillie, it is satisfying that the risk he takes translates into a just outcome. It is through moments such as these that Richard can learn that some whites will in fact treat him fairly.

Richard's move to Chicago prompts him to rethink his position on the willingness with which some blacks seem to accept their degradation. When Richard is in the South, he feels only contempt for people such as Shorty, who fully accept the degradations imposed upon them by a racist culture. However, when Richard arrives in the North, full of anxieties and uncertainties, he begins to think that "perhaps even a kick was better than uncertainty." In other words, Richard begins to have sympathy for blacks who lower their standards in order to get by. He shows that he is beginning to understand the psychic pain of the black community. He is now able to see hidden meanings rather than simply relying on the face value of actions.

Richard's anxiety about his inability to write like Proust illustrates his desire to provide a voice for the psychic pain blacks experience. Just as he hungers to gain weight to meet the postal requirement, he ravenously longs to write eloquently about the people in his environment. Richard does not desire to write fantasy stories or mystery novellas, but describes his longing to write as a "[hunger] for insight into my own life and the lives about me." Wright ends Chapter 15 by asserting that he wants to use his "fiercely indrawn nature" to the advantage of his community, not merely to his own advantage. He views writing as his responsibility to both forgive and assist the world around him. Richard also senses that his environment itself is making demands upon him, forcing him to use his silent and observant nature—which has often been his weakness—as a tool to break out of his pattern of mediocre existence and better the world around him.

PART II: CHAPTER 16

SUMMARY

Richard's intense eating regimen gives him the fifteen extra pounds he needs, and he gains the position at the post office. At work, he befriends an unnamed Irish man on the basis of their common interests, particularly their love of reading. Richard meets the Irish man's friends, and they form a casual, cynical, witty gang of Irish, black, and Jewish intellectuals. He also tries to associate with a black literary group, but finds them finicky, sex-obsessed, and superficial. Finally, Richard meets a group of Garveyites, black Americans who follow the teachings of Marcus Garvey, a black leader who advocated the return of all African-Americans to Africa to form an independent nation. The Garveyites' doctrines do not appeal to Richard, but he admires their dignity and passion.

Following the stock market crash that begins the Great Depression, Richard's hours at the post office dwindle. He loses his job entirely just when his aunt, mother, and brother fall ill. Now in dire need of a job, Richard somewhat unwillingly joins an insurance agency that exploits poor black families all over Chicago. At one point, the agency decides that their existing policies are too generous and that they must be stricter. Richard is required to participate in a con scheme: when he and the superintendent go to a home on what is supposedly a routine inspection, one of them distracts the customer, while the other switches their policy papers. Richard tries not to ponder the moral implications of his actions.

Many of the men working for the insurance company accept sex from housewives as a valid form of payment. Following their lead, Richard begins a sexual relationship with one of his clients, a single mother whose main aspiration in life is to go to the circus. Richard realizes that she is totally illiterate when she tries to read a book upside down. Richard is disgusted with her ignorance, but then becomes disgusted with himself for being disgusted with her. When Richard begins a rotation in a new neighborhood, a coworker tells him that one of the most attractive women on the route has gonorrhea. Richard later learns that his coworker was lying in order to keep the woman for himself.

During his rounds with the insurance company, Richard hears a group of Communists giving speeches in the street. As with the Garveyites, Richard respects the Communists' passion but thinks their ideas sound weak and vague. He finds their militant atheism amusing but juvenile and believes that Communism increases ignorance through the intellectual intolerance it often requires of men. Richard concludes that these black Communists do not even understand the problems of American racism, much less those of the global class system.

On election night, Richard amuses himself by writing "I PROTEST THIS FRAUD" on his ballot. Meanwhile, the Depression worsens. Richard loses his insurance job and must move to cheaper housing. Burning with shame, he forces himself to accept food donations from the government relief station, which causes him to feel spent and desperate.

ANALYSIS

Richard's stint with the corrupt insurance company shows how the burdens of life can force people to lower their ethical standards. In the preceding chapters, Richard has proven himself to be a principled person. He resists theft until despair drives him reluctantly to steal, he cares for his mother and supports his family, and he vigorously protests hypocrisy within his family and at his graduation. Numerous episodes have demonstrated that Richard has a highly developed sense of justice. Here, however, we are surprised to see him fully participate in the dirty dealings of the insurance agents, particularly their mistreatment of women and their illegal policy swaps. Before we can condemn Wright's actions too strongly, however, he is careful to outline why he chooses to work at the insurance company: "I could quit and starve. But I did not feel that being honest was worth the price of starvation." Wright suggests that at a certain point of physical desperation, ethical behavior becomes an unaffordable luxury. In a sense, this statement is an extension of Wright's assertion in Chapter 10 that black theft and dishonesty are justified in light of the unfairness of their economic arrangements with whites. Yet Wright is making a different point here. In Chapter 10, he is concerned with the survival of the entire black race in America, saying that blacks sometimes have no way to get ahead aside from defrauding their white oppressors. Here, however, Wright is more concerned with personal survival, asserting that each person's will to survive can lead to unfair action against any group, even his own race.

Richard's inability to identify fully with any of the groups he encounters in this chapter—the black literary group, the Garveyites, or the Communists—is an extension of the problems he experiences with the black community in the South. Throughout his life in the South, Richard struggles with a black culture that tries to reshape him according to what it believes he should be: in Richard's case, he should be less bookish, more obedient, and more religious. Richard has too strong a sense of self to suffer an identity imposed from without, so he eternally appears out of step with his home community. A similar situation occurs in Richard's interactions with these new groups in Chicago. In order to join the black literary group, the Garveyites, or the Communists, he must commit himself entirely to sexual obsessions, a nostalgic desire to return to Africa, or an ardent belief that revolution is the only solution. Richard cannot reduce his identity to any one idea, however, and therefore once again finds himself unable to march in step with a group.

The final paragraphs of this chapter create an apocalyptic mood. The apocalyptic writing found in the Bible describes a time of decadence, corruption, and suffering as the necessary precursor to the inauguration of God's rule on earth—in essence, an expression of the folk proverb "It's always darkest before dawn." At the end of this chapter of *Black Boy,* the new apartment to which Richard moves his family is described as "dismal," with cracking plaster and sagging stairs. Richard feels "bleak" and worries that he has not "done what I had come to the city to do." Moreover, when he finally resorts to getting food at the relief station, he feels that he has "come to the end of something." The image of the drooping, rotting apartment combines with the language of finality and despair to create an apocalyptic mood. In light of the biblical definition and the proverb about dark and dawn, this mood suggests that a significant change in Richard's life may be imminent.

PART II: CHAPTERS 17–18

SUMMARY: CHAPTER 17
While waiting in line at the relief station, Richard notes the impoverished, hungry mass of people sharing their experiences of privation and suffering. He remarks that they no longer appear to be individuals, but rather a community that could organize to throw off the oppressive forces ruling over them. Richard no longer feels that he suffers alone, realizing that millions of others are in the same lot of poverty and desperation.

Richard's cynicism vanishes. He begins to muse about revolutions and other acts of social change. He senses that the members of society most dangerous to the ruling class are not those who try to defend their rights, but rather those who have no interest in the prizes their society offers. Richard believes that black Americans fit into this inactive category of people. When whites react with violence and terror whenever blacks try to make something of their lives, they unknowingly encourage blacks to abandon any interest in social progress. Richard considers that the oppressive whites could be in great danger if blacks begin to form their own way of life as a community, as he watches them do at the relief station.

Through a federal relief program, Richard obtains a job as an orderly at a medical research institute in a wealthy hospital. He immediately notices the segregation of labor: the health professionals are all white, while the menial workers are mostly black. Richard becomes interested in the research that takes place at the hospital, but the white doctors rudely rebuff his questions.

Richard works in the hospital basement with three other black men. One, Bill, is about Richard's age, and a drunk. He terrifies Richard with his brutal ideas, at one point advocating a solution to the race problem that entails guns, bullets, and the phrase "Let us all start over again." The other two workers, Brand and Cooke, are older and passionately hate each other. Richard muses that their ignorant, narrow lives force them to invent a reason to hate each other so that they can indulge in passionate emotions.

The lab uses dogs, among other animals, for research purposes. To minimize noise in the hospital, the doctors cut the dogs' vocal cords, using a drug called Nembutal to sedate them. Upon regaining consciousness, the dogs howl silently, and Richard sees the dogs as symbols of silent suffering. He is intrigued by Nembutal and one day decides to smell a vial of it. When he does so, Brand panics, frantically yelling that Nembutal is poisonous and that they must find Richard a doctor immediately. Brand soon reveals that he is joking, but Richard is not amused.

Later, Richard's boss sends a Jewish boy to time him while he cleans, making him feel more like a slave than he ever has before. Richard grows more irritated when he is cleaning the steps and not one white employee shows him the courtesy of not stepping on the steps that he is cleaning. Dirty water gets tracked everywhere, forcing Richard to repeatedly start anew.

One day, Brand and Cooke get in a trivial argument about the weather, which eventually escalates into a physical struggle that knocks over dozens of animal cages. The four workers frantically clean up the mess, but they have no idea which animals go into which cages. They keep the accident a secret, but Wright wonders if it has destroyed any important scientific research.

Summary: Chapter 18

My life as a Negro in America had led me to feel . . .
that the problem of human unity was more important
than bread, more important than physical living
itself. . . . (See QUOTATIONS, p. 74)

Richard joins some of his friends from the post office for a political discussion, and he is surprised to discover that many of them are now members of the Communist Party. At the request of one of these friends, Richard reluctantly attends a meeting of the John Reed Club, a revolutionary artists' organization. The white members welcome him—which makes him uneasy—and invite him to attend an editorial meeting of their magazine, *Left Front*. They also give him back issues of the magazines *Masses* and *International Literature*. Richard goes home and reads these magazines through the night, greatly intrigued by their promise of worldwide unity among oppressed and suffering masses. This hopeful aspect of Communism begins to appeal to Richard, even though the movement's economic idealism and deliberately subversive message have failed to attract him before. He writes a crude, free-verse poem on revolutionary themes. When his mother reacts in horror to the fierce cartoons in the magazines, Richard realizes that the Communists have not yet found the right language for mass appeal. When he tries to discuss this deficiency at a John Reed meeting, however, a fruitless argument ensues. Richard decides that he can put his writing to use by finding the right language for speaking to the masses.

After several meetings with the John Reed Club, Richard begins to trust the motives of the white members and finally feels genuinely accepted. He begins planning a series of biographical sketches of black Communists, which he believes would help other black people understand Communism. Richard quickly detects a bitter dispute between the painters and the writers in the Club. The writers elect him executive secretary of the Club against his will, hoping to use him to expel the painters. Richard then officially joins the Communist Party. The bickering between the painters and the writers, and between the Communist Party members and the non-Party members, however, taxes the energies of Richard and the Club.

In the midst of this political turmoil, a man named Comrade Young appears and joins the Club, identifying himself as a member of the Communist Party and the Detroit John Reed Club. Young immediately accuses Swann, one of the Club's most promising artists, of being a police collaborator and enemy of the Party. Everybody assumes that Young is an important Party official, but no one can verify this assumption, so no one knows exactly what is going on. When Young disappears, the Club members search his belongings and find a note identifying him as an escapee from a Detroit mental institution, along with a dissertation titled "A Pictorial Record of Man's Economic Progress" written on a twenty-yard scroll of paper. Deeply embarrassed, Richard and the other Club officials decide to keep this information from the rest of the group.

ANALYSIS: CHAPTERS 17–18

Chapters 17 and 18 fulfill the promise of a new era in Richard's life foreshadowed by the apocalyptic mood at the end of Chapter 16. While Richard waits in the relief line, he suddenly feels the sense of community that exists between all suffering people. At the same time, he sees that others have begun to sense this kinship themselves: "their talking was enabling them to sense the collectivity of their lives." These experiences replace Richard's cynicism with hope, but he is still not quite capable of articulating this hope. He knows that it has something to do with the power and promise of needy people coming together to comprehend the meaning of their suffering and their capacity for change. Communism soon provides him with the appropriate vocabulary for expressing this hope and furnishes him with a sense of purpose as a black writer.

Richard's experiences as a hospital orderly illustrate three different forms of irony. First, narrative irony, which, as the name suggests, occurs when the mood created at one point in a narrative quickly shifts. Immediately preceding the story of his work in the hospital, Richard stands in line at the relief station, watching the black men and women talk with each other and swooning with visions of the unity of all oppressed people worldwide. From this optimistic mood, Wright immediately brings us into the hospital basement, where Brand and Cooke appear as absolute jewels of pettiness and buffoonery. Richard's vision of hope is thus ironically replaced by an immediate experience of utter hopelessness.

Second, situational irony refers to circumstances that seem the opposite of what one would expect. In these chapters, situational irony arises from the racial segregation of employees in the hospital. Richard has moved to the North because of the promise that Chicago would be free from racism. Yet he finds racism anyway—though perhaps not in as overt a form—most ironically in a hospital, a scientific institution ostensibly devoted to the public good.

Third, dramatic irony occurs when we as readers know something that a character does not. At the hospital, Richard, predictably, is interested in the research. Yet when he tries to learn about it, a doctor says to him, "If you know too much, boy, your brains might explode." These words are quite ironic, for there is a decent chance that Richard actually knows more than this snobby doctor: not about medicine, but about literature, sociology, history, politics, and other disciplines. Readers of *Black Boy* know Richard's ambitious self-education and his future as a prominent writer and intellectual. The doctor does not, which makes his words comically misguided and ironic.

Though Richard embraces Communism as a means to organize and express his hope for the unity of oppressed peoples, we immediately see hints that Communism will not be the ultimate answer he has been looking for. Richard is discouraged when the Communist cartoons horrify his mother, as he notes that it is difficult to lead the masses when addressing them in a manner that they cannot understand. Moreover, the petty bickering within the Party disheartens him, leading him to bemoan the fact that if the John Reed Club cannot unite itself, it will never be able to unite the masses. The episode with Comrade Young is perhaps the most obvious indication that Communism will not meet Richard's hopeful expectations. Young's sudden appearance and seizure of power is quite funny, but it makes Richard wonder: "what kind of club did we run that a lunatic could step into it and help run it?" He is right to ask, because this incident, more than any other, serves to undermine the integrity of the movement in which he has so much faith.

PART II: CHAPTERS 19–20

SUMMARY: CHAPTER 19

> *I would make his life more intelligible to others than it
> was to himself. I would reclaim his disordered days
> and cast them into a form that people could grasp,
> see, understand, and accept.* (See QUOTATIONS, p. 75)

Richard joins a unit of black Communists. At the first meeting, he
describes his duties at the John Reed Club, provoking giggles and
condescending remarks from his comrades. Richard soon learns
that they are mocking his eloquence: his intelligent manner of
speaking and his ambition to become a writer have branded him an
"intellectual." He also soon learns that the group disapproves of the
fact that he reads books not endorsed by the Party. Sadly, Richard
begins to understand that his comrades firmly believe that, because
Communists know the answers to all questions already, anyone
who exhibits curiosity should be viewed with suspicion. Richard
concludes that they are ignorant.

Ross, a black Communist facing legal prosecution for rioting,
consents to a series of interviews for Richard's biographical
sketches. Word of this activity spreads through the Party. A black
comrade visits Richard to warn him that intellectuals do not fit well
with the Communist Party, pointing out that the Soviet Union has
had to expel and even shoot many of them. Richard is dumbfounded and protests that he is not an intellectual. He says that he
sweeps streets for a living, and, in fact, the relief system has just
assigned him this job. Richard's visitor then suggests that a violent
confrontation with the police would bolster Richard's credibility.
Richard is dumbfounded. He cannot understand why his ambition
to write—to make black suffering intelligible and meaningful
through writing—is so controversial.

Ed Green, another black Communist, interrupts a meeting
between Ross and Richard to ask if Richard has shown his notes to
anyone else. Later, Richard learns that Green has been representing
Ross in his indictment proceedings and that he wants to know if
Richard has written anything that could be used against his client in
court. Again, Richard is dumbfounded at this suspicion. Afterward,
Ross becomes cagey and uneasy around Richard. Richard grows
increasingly frustrated, as his black comrades suspect his every

move. To make matters worse, his white comrades idealize blacks to such a degree that they cannot understand Richard's struggles with black Party members. He begins to feel an emotional isolation unlike anything he felt in the South.

Ross grows so hesitant that Richard abandons his idea of biographical sketches altogether. Instead, he decides to write a series of short stories based on the details he knows of his black comrades' lives. Suddenly, the Party charges Ross with "antileadership tendencies," "class collaborationist attitudes," and "ideological factionalism." A group of black comrades visit to inform Richard of the Party's decision that Richard must stay away from Ross. Richard tells them that he has done nothing wrong and that he feels unable to comply with the decision. They leave him, wearing cryptic smiles.

Richard finds some respite from his political anxieties by working with wild, restless boys at the South Side Boys' Club. His attempts to write short stories, however, prove frustrating. The John Reed Club organizes a conference to debate the role of writers in the Party. Richard finds the decisions aimed against writers stiff and unrealistic, but his Club comrades urge him to hitchhike to New York City to attend a similar conference. The white comrades there have trouble finding someone willing to house a black comrade, and Richard becomes disgusted. He looks for a hotel in Harlem, but finds only hotels for whites, making him even more disgusted. These troubles seem to him much more pressing than any questions about the left-wing literary movement, so he has trouble focusing on the conference. Over Richard's vehement objections, the conference moves to dissolve the John Reed Clubs due to their subversive nature as literary societies. When the final vote is taken, Richard casts the sole dissenting vote.

Richard stops attending meetings, as his duties have been eliminated along with the John Reed Clubs. He learns that a slew of lavish accusations have been leveled against him, and he prepares to quit the Party. However, Buddy Nealson, a high-ranking black comrade, calls Richard to a private meeting and convinces him to start organizing a committee against the high cost of living. Richard reluctantly accepts, even though he knows nothing about the topic and it restricts his time for writing. When the Party insists that he drop his writing completely and go to Switzerland to meet with a youth delegation, Richard asks that his membership be dropped. His request is mysteriously deferred. As Richard's comrades continue to slander him, Richard realizes that they are trying to keep him in the Party so as to assassinate his character and expel him themselves.

The relief authorities install Richard as the publicity agent for the Federal Negro Theater. He recruits a talented Jewish director. Together, they try to persuade the actors to perform works that realistically depict the experiences of black Americans. The black actors, accustomed to vaudeville and musical comedy, resist performing in such a controversial work. In fact, they go so far as to violently demand that the director be fired. When Richard talks in private with the director about how to remedy the situation, the actors brand Richard the "white man's nigger" and threaten him with knives. Frightened and disgusted, Richard has the Works Progress Administration transfer him to a white experimental theater company.

At the request of some comrades, Richard attends the Party meeting at which Ross goes on trial for a long list of offenses. To establish the context for Ross's crimes, the trial begins with several speakers who give a detailed picture of oppressed peoples worldwide. The moral force of the presentation stuns Richard. He views the trial as a spectacle of glory, as Ross achieves unity with his comrades by confessing his crimes and asking forgiveness. On the other hand, Richard views the trial as a spectacle of horror, because it implicitly condemns Richard himself. He leaves the trial before it ends, and his former comrades shun him thereafter.

Summary: Chapter 20

The relief station transfers Richard to the Federal Writers' Project, but the Communists who work with him there agitate for his removal. When his boss tells him not to worry, Richard learns that the Communists had also been responsible for his difficulties at the Federal Negro Theater. With the Communists trying to oust him from his work, Richard decides that reconciliation with the Party is necessary. However, no Party representative will meet with him.

When Richard tries to be part of the May Day parade, he cannot find the group with which he is supposed to march. When a former comrade spots him and encourages him to march with his old comrades, Richard hesitantly agrees. Soon, however, two white Communists pick Richard up and throw him out of the parade, while his black comrades only look on sheepishly. He walks home, angry and bleeding from his fall, convinced that the Communists have been blinded by oppression. Richard believes that mankind can learn only slowly and painfully and that now he must "build a bridge of words" between himself and the outside world.

ANALYSIS: CHAPTERS 19–20

Richard's independent personality makes his conflict with the domineering Communist Party seem inevitable. As with so many other problematic relationships in Richard's life—with his family, with Southern whites, with his school principal—his confrontation with the Communist Party stems in large part from his incredibly strong sense of self. Though he has sometimes feared that his insecurity and self-loathing would get the better of him, for the most part he has followed his own interests and played by his own rules regardless of the cost. Such an individual temperament is incompatible with Communism's emphasis on conformity, so anyone possessed of such a temperament is bound to be a very poor Communist.

Indeed, Richard's first encounters with Communism foreshadow his eventual troubles with the Party. As we have seen in the preceding chapters, Richard finds many aspects of Communism—especially its economic policies and its more militant supporters—less than satisfying. Nonetheless, the emphasis Communism places on the unity of suffering peoples, along with the John Reed Club's initial acceptance of writers, appeals to Richard's passionate nature to change the world through his art. Notable, however, is the fact that we never read of any aspects of Communism that truly appeal to Richard's intellect. Because Richard enters the Party based on his passion and not his intellect, any commitment he makes to the Party is bound to be fraught with his independent, critical, dissenting thoughts and feelings.

Whereas Richard has spent much of *Black Boy* either running away from troubles or reacting to them cynically or unproductively, the closing scene shows that he now has a more positive outlook on life. Richard's travails with the Party could have proven supremely disheartening and debilitating for him. Motivated by high idealism, Richard has sincerely desired to unite the suffering peoples of the world and affect change through Communism. As he becomes immersed in the imperfect politics of Party life, frustration and bewilderment begin to displace his hopes, culminating with his personal condemnation and his physical ousting from the May Day parade. Richard could easily give up or succumb to paralyzing cynicism in the face of such a turn of events. However, rather than debilitating himself through self-loathing—as he does when he quits his jobs with Mr. Crane and with the Hoffmans—he now has enough self-confidence and self-respect to trust that he will find a way to work through his troubles. Richard uses his troubles to achieve a new understanding of humanity, saying, "perhaps that is the way it has always been with man. . . ." Moreover, rather than berating himself as a failure, he reaches a positive decision on how to proceed within the less-than-ideal world: Richard says he will proceed as an artist, "with no vaulting dream of achieving a vast unity." He develops a sense of himself within an imperfect world, lowering his expectations in order to give himself the power to persevere.

Richard has finally come to think of himself as a thinker-artist, accepting the difficulties and limitations associated with such a profession. His independent, challenging, and creative tendencies have always caused him trouble, but he hopes that things will be different in Chicago. He hopes to find an environment more accepting of his love of reading, learning, and writing. Yet, even in the more cosmopolitan setting of Chicago, Richard's reading chafes his family, annoys his employers, and provokes suspicion among his Communist peers. Instead of despairing, however, Richard reaches a new understanding of the imperfect world that surrounds him, and of his place in that world as a thinker-artist. He knows that he will never find an environment totally in tune with his fiercely inquisitive and creative nature. When he writes of his determination to "hurl words into this darkness and wait for an echo," Richard seems settled on a vision of himself as a thinker-artist fundamentally at odds with his world, "this darkness." After all, if he lived in an environment that embraced him fully, he would no longer need to challenge that world through writing. Instead, within this imperfect world Richard must create challenging, insightful works of art, throwing them into the environment to "wait for an echo," an indication that what he says has resonated with someone, somewhere. As with many artists, Richard's artistic sense of duty might lead to a lonely existence, but perhaps his commitment to that duty is what carries Wright to the artistic maturity needed to write his great novels.

IMPORTANT QUOTATIONS EXPLAINED

1.   At the age of twelve, before I had had one full year of
      formal schooling, I had . . . a conviction that the
      meaning of living came only when one was struggling
      to wring a meaning out of meaningless suffering. At
      the age of twelve I had an attitude toward life that was
      to . . . make me skeptical of everything while seeking
      everything, tolerant of all and yet critical . . . that
      could only keep alive in me that enthralling sense of
      wonder and awe in the face of the drama of human
      feeling which is hidden by the external drama of life.

These passages follow Ella's second paralytic stroke at the end of
Chapter 3. Wright illustrates many of his major ideas and beliefs
here. Principal among these is his all-important conviction that life
becomes meaningful only when we struggle to make it so. This perspective gives no intrinsic significance to life, but asserts that we can
be noble when we try to make life significant in our own way. This
point of view recalls the thinking of existentialist philosophers such
as Jean-Paul Sartre, whom Wright later read and admired. In this
passage Wright also emphasizes the paradoxical nature of his character: he is tolerant yet critical, skeptical yet seeking, timid yet head-
strong, and modest yet blindingly intelligent.

QUOTATIONS

2. I concluded the book with the conviction that I had
    somehow overlooked something terribly important in
    life. I had once tried to write, had once reveled in
    feeling, had let my crude imagination roam, but the
    impulse to dream had been slowly beaten out of me by
    experience. Now it surged up again and I hungered for
    books, new ways of looking and seeing.

This passage appears near the beginning of Chapter 13, immediately
after Richard reads H. L. Mencken's *A Book of Prefaces*. This reading of Mencken serves as a fiery baptism for Richard—it reminds
him that he has an imagination, and that his imagination is hungry.
In this sense, it marks an instance of the blurring between Richard's
desire to eat and his desire to read. This is something of a turning
point in the novel: before this point, it is unclear where Richard is
going in his life. Once or twice he mentions a fleeting desire to write,
but by the time he arrives in Memphis it seems that his interest in
reading and writing has been thoroughly extinguished. After this
point, as Richard becomes more and more dedicated to the written
word, his life achieves a more definite focus. As such, this point in
Chapter 13 could be called the climax of the novel.

3. Our too-young and too-new America . . . insists upon
   seeing the world in terms of good and bad, the holy
   and the evil, the high and the low, the white and the
   black. . . . It hugs the easy way of damning those
   whom it cannot understand, of excluding those who
   look different, and it salves its conscience with a
   self-draped cloak of righteousness. Am I damning
   my native land? No; for I, too, share these faults
   of character!

This passage appears in the middle of Chapter 15, as Richard
sketches some of the faults he finds in America. His greatest com-
plaint is that his country is superficial and self-deceptive, qualities
that result in intolerance and exclusion. When Richard admits that
he shares "these faults of character," however, he compares America
to a person like himself, growing up and working through the growing pains of adolescence. Indeed, Wright refers to the "too-young"
America, and immediately after this passage calls America "adolescent and cocksure." Richard discerns these traits in America
because he knows what it is like to be cocksure and adolescent himself. In his view, the problem of racism does not lie entirely in such
private places as peoples' minds. Rather, it is a function of problems
deeply embedded in American culture that will take time to change.

4.   My life as a Negro in America had led me to
     feel . . . that the problem of human unity was
     more important than bread, more important than
     physical living itself; for I felt that without a common
     bond uniting men . . . there could be no living worthy
     of being called human.

This passage, from the beginning of Chapter 18, appears just after
Richard returns from his first meeting with the John Reed Club.
Richard muses that, judging from his experience, the fundamental
problem of social existence is a lack of "human unity," not the need
for physical food for individual survival. To Richard, Communism,
with its focus on the masses, the unity of oppressed peoples, and
equality across all lines of race and gender, appears dedicated to
solving precisely this problem. Richard feels a spiritual connection
with Communism and feels almost as if it has brought him a spiritual awakening.

5.   I would make his life more intelligible to others than it
was to himself. I would reclaim his disordered days
and cast them into a form that people could grasp, see,
understand, and accept.

These lines, which occur near the beginning of Chapter 19, describe
Richard's motivation for his biographical sketch of Ross, the black
Communist. Richard regards life in general as a fundamentally
meaningless swirl of pain and suffering. To him, the most exciting
experiences in life are attempts to create from this chaos something
with form and order—in his case, writing, ideas, and art. But Richard
is not a vain intellectual, and does not want to sit at home and read
books for his private pleasure while the world suffers. Rather, as we
see in his attraction to the ideals of Communism, he is profoundly
concerned with the fates of other people. Richard's faith in creative
art and his concern for the public good come together in this passage.
He wants to reclaim and reinterpret his "disordered days" not just
for the private joy of creation, but also so that other people can
understand and accept what he creates. Moreover, this passage out-
lines the outcomes Richard believes biographical writing can accomplish, offering insight into what Wright hoped to accomplish with the
writing of *Black Boy*: to reorder his own past and come to understand himself, not merely for his own sake, but for our sake as well.

KEY FACTS

FULL TITLE

Black Boy (American Hunger): A Record of Childhood and Youth

AUTHOR

Richard Wright

TYPE OF WORK

Autobiographical novel

GENRE

Bildungsroman (coming-of age-novel); modernist novel; existential novel

LANGUAGE

English

TIME AND PLACE WRITTEN

1943–1944; New York City

DATE OF FIRST PUBLICATION

1945

PUBLISHER

Harper & Brothers

NARRATOR

Black Boy is narrated by the author, Richard Wright, and tells the story of his life from early childhood to about age twenty-nine.

POINT OF VIEW

As the text is written as a stylized memoir, the narrator always speaks in the first person. Although he occasionally speculates as to what another character thinks or feels, those speculations are always conditioned by the fact that the narrator is a real historical figure with limited knowledge.

TONE

Confessional, ironic, philosophical

TENSE
> Past

SETTING (TIME)
> Roughly 1912–1937

SETTING (PLACE)
> Primarily Jackson, Mississippi; West Helena and Elaine, Arkansas; Memphis, Tennessee; and Chicago, Illinois, with detours to rural areas in the Deep South and to New York City

PROTAGONIST
> Richard Wright, the author and narrator

MAJOR CONFLICT
> Richard demonstrates inborn individualism and intelligence, traits that can only cause problems for a black man in the Jim Crow South; he struggles with blacks and whites alike for acceptance and humane treatment; he struggles with his own stubborn nature.

RISING ACTION
> Ella (the schoolteacher) tells Richard the story of *Bluebeard and His Seven Wives*; Richard writes his story "The Voodoo of Hell's Half-Acre"; Richard graduates from public school and enters the workforce only to be terrorized by the actions of racist whites.

CLIMAX
> Richard reads H. L. Mencken's *A Book of Prefaces* and becomes obsessed with reading and writing; Richard permanently flees the South; he makes his way to Chicago, where he can live a more dignified life and more fully exercise his ambition to become a writer.

FALLING ACTION
> Richard comes to understand the psychic pain of growing up black in America and realizes his duty to record his experiences and his environment through writing; he enters the Communist Party and W.P.A. programs, coming into contact with serious writers and outlets for writing about his ideals; he is ousted from the Party but comes to a new vision of himself as an artist

KEY FACTS

THEMES
The insidious effects of racism; the individual versus society; the redemptive power of art

MOTIFS
Hunger; reading; violence

SYMBOLS
Ella's infirmity; the Memphis optical shop

FORESHADOWING
Perhaps the sharpest foreshadowing in the novel is the activity of Comrade Young in the Communist Party. The fact that a madman participates in the workings of the Party without being detected suggests that the Party is fallible. Another example is Richard's relationship with his family, a relationship that foreshadows how his personality will conflict with white authority.

KEY FACTS

Study Questions & Essay Topics

Study Questions

1.   *Why do you think Wright titled his autobiography*
     Black Boy?

The word "boy" in the title seems logical, on the one hand, because Wright's autobiography is clearly the story of his childhood. On the other hand, the use of "boy" is ironic, as the story covers a time period extending far beyond the stage in life when males are considered boys. Wright's story ends with an important realization about his identification as an artist. In this context, he may be using the title to imply that, though he goes through adolescence and attains physical adulthood earlier in the novel, he is emotionally still a boy until he reaches this awareness at the end of the narrative. Prior to this final realization, Richard is still young, inexperienced, and unable to come to terms with his place in the world around him. As such, the title highlights the ironic fact that, despite his precocious tendencies to educate himself, Richard remains inexperienced until he finally makes his key realization as an adult. In drawing attention to his slow growth into manhood, Wright implies that the world in which he grew up—both the white and the black communities—failed to educate him properly and provide him with adequate opportunities to gain confidence in his individuality and identity.

Wright's choice of title also casts his autobiography as a commentary on racism in America. He does not simply use the word "boy," but qualifies it with the word "black," indicating that his childhood and growth are inseparable from the influences of racism in America. Wright must identify himself as "black" in the title because that is how his childhood environment forces him to think of himself—not as a person, but always as a black person.

Additionally, the word "boy" has racist resonances; it is especially associated with Southern whites who wish to degrade black men by implying that they are incapable of growing into real men. Throughout his autobiography, Richard is commonly addressed as "boy"—especially in the South, but even in the North. Yet we see that Richard grows into his manhood and identity with a maturity that surpasses that of the people around him. Seen this way, Wright's use of "boy" in the title may be ironic. In any case, despite its two-word simplicity, the title is open to different interpretations and can define his autobiography in many ways. The second edition of the novel contains an alternative title or subtitle, *American Hunger*, indicating that Wright wishes to emphasize the theme of literal and figurative hunger as much the theme of racism.

2.   *Why does Richard's family treat him so harshly? How does this treatment affect our impression of the family?*

In part, Richard's family treats him harshly simply because he truly offends them. Most of his family members ascribe to rigid and arbitrary sets of principles of one sort of another. When they demand that Richard adhere to these principles, he often refuses to submit, leaving him to face the consequences. Another reason for the family's harsh treatment of Richard is that his actions sometimes pose a genuine threat to them. In the novel's environment, the Jim Crow South, many whites have no qualms about punishing black insubordination with severe violence or even death. Moreover, many whites have no qualms about extending such violence to relatives and other blacks close to the offending party. We see the genuine nature of this threat of punishment-by-association when Richard and his family flee after the murder of Uncle Hoskins. They have to flee because the whites who murdered Hoskins have also threatened to kill his family. Given such dire threats, an insubordinate boy such as Richard, who could easily provoke the whites' hostility, is indeed a grave liability.

These two possible explanations for the family's harsh treatment of Richard evoke markedly different sympathies in us as readers. The idea that Richard's family is merely forcing him to conform to their personal beliefs evokes sympathy for Richard only, as it depicts him as a hapless victim of dictatorial whims. The second explanation—that Richard poses a threat to the family's safety—is quite tragic, as the threat of violence from outside drives the family to do violence to itself. This explanation evokes sympathy for the entire family—indeed, for the entire black community. Whether Wright himself wishes to sympathize with his family is, of course, a matter of interpretation, but he implicitly criticizes the black community for failing to strengthen itself so that it can nurture its more undisciplined members rather than beat them. This is not to say that Wright fails to recognize that it is the insidious effect of racism that breeds violence in his family—indeed, he recognizes this relationship undeniably. However, Wright also implies that all people, including the black community, must face the difficult task of overcoming such injustice, rather than succumbing to it by resorting to weakness.

3.   *Discuss the role of art in Richard's life. How does Richard talk about art? Does he value art? What significance do Richard's feelings about art have for an overall interpretation of* Black Boy?

Richard's relationship with art begins when he hears Ella the schoolteacher's telling of the plot of *Bluebeard and His Seven Wives,* an event that elicits what Richard calls his first "total emotional response." When Granny rushes out and interrupts this moment, she symbolically brings religion into conflict with art. From that point forward, Richard's relationship with art, which is manifest in his desire to read, develops in contrast to his relationship with religion, which he sees as an inferior opposing force. Art in effect *becomes* Richard's religion, his only spiritual outlet. He often speaks of art with language normally associated with religious experience, further suggesting that Richard regards art as a substitute for religion—that is, as an alternate mode of redemption. Such a belief accords with his view that meaning comes only from an attempt to make meaning. To redeem oneself is to create—through art, in Richard's case—as much order and meaning in one's life as possible. Perhaps the ultimate achievement along these lines is to write one's autobiography and impose order upon the whole of one's experience. In this sense, we might attribute the very existence of *Black Boy* itself to Richard's deep sensitivity to the meaning of art.

SUGGESTED ESSAY TOPICS

1. Describe the evolution of Richard's attitude toward white people. At what points do we detect a shift in his attitude?

2. In what ways does Wright, as an adult writing his autobiography in retrospect, color the description of events and experiences as they unfold?

3. Discuss Richard's thoughts on stealing. How does he justify it? Does his justification of stealing imply a justification for the violent way his family treats him as a child?

4. Richard's mature character is formed both by the kind of knowledge only gained through experience in the world and by the kind of knowledge only gained through reading books. With respect to Richard, does one of these types of knowledge seem more important than the other? Why or why not?

5. What role does hunger play in the autobiography? How does Richard view hunger at the end of the novel? Has his attitude changed?

REVIEW & RESOURCES

QUIZ

1. In his childhood and early youth, how does Richard react to the submission of other black Americans to white authority?

    A. With contemptuous astonishment
    B. With understanding
    C. With approval
    D. With amusement

2. What is Granny's religious affiliation?

    A. Southern Baptist
    B. Methodist
    C. Seventh-Day Adventist
    D. Unitarian

3. Which statement accurately describes Richard's relationship with Granny?

    A. It is affectionate
    B. It is practically nonexistent, since they rarely interact
    C. They do not have a relationship, as she died before his birth
    D. It is filled with conflict and hostility

4. Which of the following best describes Richard's education?

    A. It is entirely self-acquired
    B. It consists of some formal schooling and lots of self-directed reading
    C. He has only an elementary-school education
    D. He has a high-school education

5. How does Richard react to his mother's first stroke?

    A. He begins to feel that the world is a hostile place
    B. He becomes extremely religious because the church offers him comfort and security
    C. He develops close ties with the black community and his family because they offer emotional and financial support
    D. He becomes depressed and suicidal

6. Which of the following best describes Richard's childhood?

    A. It is characterized by grinding poverty
    B. It is characterized by isolation and loneliness
    C. It is characterized by frequent, sudden moves
    D. All of the above

7. What is Richard's adult attitude toward his father?

    A. Hateful
    B. Pitying
    C. Fearful
    D. Loving

8. Who is Richard's favorite aunt?

    A. Addie
    B. Cleo
    C. Maggie
    D. Jody

9. Which of the following best describes Richard's relationship with his mother?

    A. Frequently conflicted, but she is the most loving, supportive member of his family
    B. Rife with conflict and hostility
    C. Entirely loving and supportive
    D. Cold and uneasy

10. Who is Richard's only source of encouragement when he publishes his first story in the local newspaper?

    A. His mother
    B. The newspaper editor
    C. His school principal
    D. Aunt Maggie

11. What happens when Richard enters the working world?

    A. He is harassed and abused by his white coworkers
    B. He is fired for not acting properly
    C. He comes to better understand why many black Americans submit to white authority
    D. All of the above

12. Why does Richard succumb to stealing?

    A. To earn money to leave the South
    B. He thinks stealing is cool
    C. To gain his coworkers' approval
    D. All of the above

13. Why is Richard unable to check books out of the Memphis public library?

    A. The librarian is racist and denies his application for a library card
    B. None of Richard's coworkers will loan him a library card
    C. The public library does not allow black people borrowing privileges
    D. Richard gets lost every time he goes looking for the library

14. How does Richard feel when he first arrives in Chicago?

    A. Frightened and bewildered
    B. Homesick for the South
    C. Overjoyed
    D. Calm and collected

REVIEW & RESOURCES

15. What does Richard think of the Hoffmans?

    A.   He hates them because they are Jewish
    B.   He assumes they are like Southern white people
    C.   He thinks they make him work too hard
    D.   He finds them stupid and overbearing

16. What political organization does Richard join in Chicago?

    A.   The Garveyites
    B.   The Democratic Party
    C.   The Communist Party
    D.   The Fascist Party

17. For what job does Richard have to gain weight?

    A.   His job as a street sweeper
    B.   His job as broncobuster at a Wyoming ranch
    C.   His job at the sawmill
    D.   His job in the post office

18. Who is Comrade Young?

    A.   A high-ranking official in the Communist Party
    B.   A hostile spy in the Communist Party
    C.   An escapee from a Detroit mental institution
    D.   A promising artist whom the Communist Party puts
         on trial

19. How do the black Communists react to Richard's desire
    to write?

    A.   With condescension
    B.   With distrust
    C.   With fear
    D.   All of the above

20. Which of the following best describes Richard's attraction to the Communist Party?

    A. He likes its philosophical outlook but has trouble with its paranoia and intransigence

    B. He believes the Party is fundamentally racist

    C. He is brainwashed into accepting its dogma

    D. He treats it as an amusing joke

21. Which statement accurately describes Richard's experience with the actors at the Federal Negro Theater?

    A. He develops close ties with them that become the first lasting relationships of his life

    B. He is frustrated by their resistance to controversial productions that examine the reality of racism in America

    C. He leaves the job because they harshly criticize his writing

    D. None of the above

22. How does Richard's mother react to the cartoon she sees in one of Richard's Communist magazines?

    A. It makes her concerned that Richard has been brainwashed

    B. It makes her want to join the Party

    C. She finds it grotesque and horrible

    D. It strikes her as peculiarly childish

23. How are Richard's experiences with the Communist Party similar to his experiences with Granny?

    A. Both Granny and the Party disapprove of his desire to write

    B. Both Granny and the Party disapprove of his love of reading

    C. Both Granny and the Party try to force him to accept rigid dogma

    D. All of the above

24. How does Richard describe Ross's trial?

    A. Glorious
    B. Horrific
    C. Both horrific and glorious
    D. Tedious and uneventful

25. How does Richard react to his final rejection by the Communist Party?

    A. He seeks out John Rockefeller and becomes a devout capitalist
    B. He despairs that, without an intellectually nurturing community, he has no hope for a writing career
    C. He thinks that the charges leveled against him are accurate
    D. His determination to write and to do things his own way despite the challenges grows stronger than ever

SUGGESTIONS FOR FURTHER READING

BRIGNANO, RUSSELL C. *Richard Wright: An Introduction to the Man and His Works*. Pittsburgh: University of Pittsburgh Press, 1972.

FABRE, MICHEL. *The World of Richard Wright*. Jackson: University Press of Mississippi, 1985.

GATES, HENRY LOUIS, JR. and K. A. APPIAH, eds. *Richard Wright: Critical Perspectives Past and Present*. New York: Amistad, 1993.

HAKUTANI, YOSHINOBU, ed. *Critical Essays on Richard Wright*. Boston: G. K. Hall, 1982.

KINNAMON, KENETH. *The Emergence of Richard Wright: A Study of Literature and Society*. Urbana: University of Illinois Press, 1973.

MARGOLIES, EDWARD. *The Art of Richard Wright*. Carbondale: Southern Illinois University Press, 1969.

MILLER, EUGENE E. *Voice of a Native Son: The Poetics of Richard Wright*. Jackson: University Press of Mississippi, 1990.

RAMPERSAD, ARNOLD, ed. *Richard Wright: A Collection of Critical Essays*. Englewood Cliffs, New Jersey: Prentice Hall, 1995.

REVIEW & RESOURCES

SparkNotes Study Guides:

1984
The Adventures of
  Huckleberry Finn
The Adventures of
  Tom Sawyer
The Aeneid
All Quiet on the
  Western Front
And Then There
  Were None
Angela's Ashes
Animal Farm
Anne of Green Gables
Antony and Cleopatra
As I Lay Dying
As You Like It
The Awakening
The Bean Trees
The Bell Jar
Beloved
Beowulf
Billy Budd
Black Boy
Bless Me, Ultima
The Bluest Eye
Brave New World
The Brothers
  Karamazov
The Call of the Wild
Candide
The Canterbury Tales
Catch-22
The Catcher in the Rye
The Chosen
Cold Mountain
Cold Sassy Tree
The Color Purple
The Count of
  Monte Cristo
Crime and Punishment
The Crucible
Cry, the Beloved
  Country
Cyrano de Bergerac
Death of a Salesman

The Diary of a
  Young Girl
Doctor Faustus
A Doll's House
Don Quixote
Dr. Jekyll and Mr. Hyde
Dracula
Dune
Emma
Ethan Frome
Fahrenheit 451
Fallen Angels
A Farewell to Arms
Flowers for Algernon
The Fountainhead
Frankenstein
The Glass Menagerie
Gone With the Wind
The Good Earth
The Grapes of Wrath
Great Expectations
The Great Gatsby
Gulliver's Travels
Hamlet
The Handmaid's Tale
Hard Times
Harry Potter and the
  Sorcerer's Stone
Heart of Darkness
Henry IV, Part I
Henry V
Hiroshima
The Hobbit
The House of the
  Seven Gables
I Know Why the
  Caged Bird Sings
The Iliad
Inferno
Invisible Man
Jane Eyre
Johnny Tremain
The Joy Luck Club
Julius Caesar
The Jungle

The Killer Angels
King Lear
The Last of the
  Mohicans
Les Misérables
A Lesson Before
  Dying
The Little Prince
Little Women
Lord of the Flies
Macbeth
Madame Bovary
A Man for All Seasons
The Mayor of
  Casterbridge
The Merchant of
  Venice
A Midsummer
  Night's Dream
Moby-Dick
Much Ado About
  Nothing
My Ántonia
Mythology
Native Son
The New Testament
Night
The Odyssey
The Oedipus Trilogy
Of Mice and Men
The Old Man and
  the Sea
The Old Testament
Oliver Twist
The Once and
  Future King
One Flew Over the
  Cuckoo's Nest
One Hundred Years
  of Solitude
Othello
Our Town
The Outsiders
Paradise Lost
The Pearl

The Picture of
  Dorian Gray
A Portrait of the Artist
  as a Young Man
Pride and Prejudice
The Prince
A Raisin in the Sun
The Red Badge of
  Courage
The Republic
Richard III
Robinson Crusoe
Romeo and Juliet
The Scarlet Letter
A Separate Peace
Silas Marner
Sir Gawain and the
  Green Knight
Slaughterhouse-Five
Snow Falling on Cedars
The Sound and the Fury
Steppenwolf
The Stranger
A Streetcar Named
  Desire
The Sun Also Rises
A Tale of Two Cities
The Taming of
  the Shrew
The Tempest
Tess of the
  d'Urbervilles
Their Eyes Were
  Watching God
Things Fall Apart
To Kill a Mockingbird
To the Lighthouse
Treasure Island
Twelfth Night
Ulysses
Uncle Tom's Cabin
Walden
Wuthering Heights
A Yellow Raft in
  Blue Water